Barren Earth
to
New Growth

Triduum

Sunday of the Lord's Resurrection

Feasts Following Easter

Cycles A-B-C

Alonso de Blas, O.F.M.

Tau publishing
Phoenix, Arizona

Book Layout and Design: Arlene Besore
Image Credit: Jeffrey Campbell

Copyright © 2006 Tau-publishing—Phoenix Arizona
First Edition February 2007

For re-orders and other inspirational books and materials:
Tau-publishing.com

ISBN 978-0-9719921-8-4   Perfect Bound
ISBN 978-0-9719921-9-1   Case Bound

Unless a wheat grain falls into the earth and dies,

It remains only a single grain;

But if it dies

It yields a rich harvest.

John 12:24

For my family:

Dad and Mom and all my relatives

My Franciscan brothers

All who have made me a part of their lives

Contents

One
GENERAL INTRODUCTION

T raditionally, when we depicted the seasons of the liturgical year we did so in a pie chart, with slices representing each season (some narrower, some wider) in its appropriate color: purple for Lent, green for Ordinary Time, etc. Remember the bulletin boards that our grammar school teachers used? These days, having recovered the early Church's point of view, we more accurately present the church year in the form of a solar system. The Easter Triduum (Three-Days) isn't just another slice of the pie, it is the sun-center that provides light and cohesive meaning to the other seasons in orbit around it. (This lovely and super-appropriate image appears in the Spring 1979 AIM, "Easter Triduum – Spirit and Observance," by Rev. Jerome Siwek, p.4.) The central observance and celebration of the entire church year must be this Easter

Triduum, which begins on Holy Thursday evening and concludes on the Great Vigil of Easter or, by extension, on Easter Sunday.

This solar model allows us to re-judge the many practices that popular devotion had tacked on over the centuries. Notice that by definition Lent is over by Holy Thursday morning—that evening begins the Easter Triduum. That's why we shouldn't find celebrations of the sacrament of reconciliation at this time, because they belong to the spirituality of Lent. The Easter Triduum is not a time for reconciliation/penance, but for the prayerful consideration and celebration of our most important feast: the dying and rising of Jesus. [By the way: the word is pronounced "tree-doo-oom" as if taking two syllables to say the word "doom."]

In 1955 Pope Pius XII restored Holy Week (the "Week of Salvation" as the Eastern Church calls it) to the prominence it had in ancient times, a prominence largely lost in our day not only because changed social conditions no longer allowed people to attend the services in great numbers, but also because people had lost sight of the true nature of the events being commemorated. (Remember Mass of the Dead with black vestments, dark orange candles at the catafalque, and spooky music?)

Notice how the liturgists were ahead of the bishops: a decade before Vatican II, the Easter Triduum was restored as the heart of the church's year. Through the rites of Holy Week we relive the central mystery of our redemption. This pastoral consideration prompted the Pope to insist on the active participation of the people in the Holy Week liturgies so that the whole church could be drawn into the celebration of Christ's saving death and rising.

In order to enter fully into the mystery and meaning of Easter, we should really celebrate the Triduum <u>as a whole</u>, not picking and choosing a Way of the Cross here, or a Seven Last Words there, as time allows. Ideally, you <u>make</u> time for these high holy days, and take part in the liturgy of each of these three days. The last three days of Holy Week are not simply preparations for Easter Sunday. They are gathered into a Triduum so as to show clearly that the Lord's Passover forms a continuum, from his farewell dinner, through his passion and death, to his resurrected new life, a bridge from his life with us to life with his Father and ours.

The Easter event includes both death and resurrection. Remember how already in Advent we saw that the manger and the cross were never that far apart? Both ends of Jesus' life tie together in a wonderful divine yin/yang. It's as if the Father is telling us: "I've got some happy news and some sad news...but don't worry—it's all good!" Now the Triduum presents the same concept, but in reverse—from crushingly sad to gloriously joyful, presenting the passion, death, and rising of Jesus as a continuum: from cruel suffering, through an ignominious death, to a glorious, never-ending risen life. The liturgies of Holy Thursday and Good Friday contain numerous references to the resurrection, while that of Easter alludes to the passion and death of Jesus. "The church speaks of these days not as days of sorrow, but of prayerful meditation, reflection and celebration of the one event—the dying and rising of Jesus" (Fr. Siwek, p.5). On these high holy days prayer, silence, time for reading and reflection, rest and joining in worship should push aside our daily activities and our normal preoccupations.

There are Catholics who are not familiar with the special services celebrated during Holy Week. They have avoided them because they are "different" (read: "long"). But doesn't any event that is special for us usually call for a change in our routine? Thanksgiving dinner takes a lot longer than ordinary Thursday dinners, but isn't that the point? And, in case you were wondering, for centuries the days of the Triduum were "Holy Days of Obligation" until Pope Urban VIII changed them in 1642. That may not have been such a bad move: our willingness to enter into these mysteries should certainly trace back not to a sense of obligation, but to a loving appreciation of what it means to us today that Christ died and rose to new life—for Christians, the most important event in all of history.

Holy Week opens with "Palm Sunday," one of the principal days of the year on which the number of people in attendance increases noticeably. (Could it be because they're finally getting something, for a change?) (Just kidding…I think.) How does this anticipation of the Triduum relate? It's a sort of preview, it alerts us to what we will be about later in the week. Ideally, it is a Triduum-in-miniature, since the liturgy addresses all the events (the suffering, dying and rising) of Easter, but in an abbreviated form.

"Entrance" is the theme of this special Sunday. The church celebrates Christ's entrance into Jerusalem to begin the fulfillment of
the paschal mystery. We enter into Jerusalem with Christ, into our
holiest week, into our final stages of journeying with him. Today
we celebrate "entrance." Ordinarily, we file into church as we
arrive—one by one, family by family. But today we make a grand
entrance: the entire community gathers outside and then enters
in procession. As we do, one of the gospel accounts of Jesus'
triumphant entrance into David's city is proclaimed. And, moving
with Jesus, we enter into the gospel. "The crowd...cut branches
from the trees and strewed them on the road. [Those] preceding
him and those following kept crying out 'Hosanna to the Son
of David; blessed is he who comes in the name of the Lord;
hosanna in the highest'" (Mt. 21:8-10). This is one of the most
joyful and triumphant processions of our whole church year. We
carry palm branches, in many countries woven with decorative
ribbons and flowers. We enter singing, another sign of visible
unity and shared joy.

But this is a Sunday of contrasts. As soon as our welcoming
prayer is ended, the initial reading from chapter 50 of Isaiah shifts
the mood sharply, from the glorious Son of David, to the Suffering
Servant of Yahweh who gives himself fearlessly, confident that the
Lord will be his help. The second reading, the great hymn from
Philippians 2:6-11, describes Christ emptying himself, "becoming
obedient to death, even death on a cross" but as a result, receiving exaltation from the Father, who "bestowed on him the name
that is above every name, that at the name of Jesus every knee

should bend...and every tongue confess that Jesus Christ is Lord, to the glory of the Father."

The gospel for this Sunday is so central to the liturgy that it names the whole day: Passion (Palm) Sunday. Every year one of the synoptic gospel accounts of the passion and death of Jesus is read (Cycles A, B, C/Matthew, Mark, Luke—John's passion account is always on Good Friday, regardless of the cycle). As we listen to the passion story we enter into it: we are going with Christ to Calvary and end up at the foot of his cross. Some churches, to help make the story come alive, have several people reading the parts: the narrator who moves the action along, the voice of Jesus, the voices of the individuals in the gospel account. Often the whole assembly is invited to proclaim the words of the crowd in the story—reminding us that it's our story.

Not long after filling the air with "Hosanna!" we will be calling out "crucify him!" The contrast is striking so that we can't forget that this is all too often the story of our lives: first we're full of good resolutions and the next thing we know we've given in to temptation and are among those who crucify Jesus by our sins. The church hopes that by "entering" more thoughtfully the celebration of Passion Sunday and the Triduum, we can follow Jesus more meaningfully and become better disciples as a result.

Holy Thursday, Good Friday and Holy Saturday are so unique that they have come to be known simply as the "Three Days" or Triduum. It was not always thus. In the thinking of St. Augustine

(5th century) it referred to Friday, Saturday and Sunday, "the Triduum of Christ crucified, buried, and risen," in his words. Holy Thursday was the day for the reconciliation of public penitents. For many years it was the custom to confess one's sins at the beginning of Lent—ashes being a sign of repentance. Then the rest of Lent was devoted to carrying out the penance, the most notorious (public) sinners usually sitting at the doors of the church in sackcloth and ashes, asking those who went in to remember them and pray for God's mercy on them. On Holy Thursday the penitents were finally reconciled to God and could re-enter the church, to enter fully into the Triduum celebration (Good Friday, Holy Saturday and Easter Sunday) by sharing the Eucharist, the assembly's family meal, at the family table.

Not long after the time of Augustine, the church in Rome began to celebrate a special commemoration of the Last Supper of the Lord on the Thursday evening before Good Friday, and ever since the Triduum has been considered to refer to Holy Thursday, Good Friday and Holy Saturday, with the rising of Christ happening during the night before the dawn of Easter Sunday.

[For much of the presentation regarding Palm Sunday I'm greatly indebted to Thomas Richstatter, O.F.M.'s April 1992 Catholic Update "Our Holiest Week."]

Two
TRIDUUM – HOLY THURSDAY

Historical Background:
The Jewish Feast of Passover

S cholars claim this is an ancient feast, dating back to before the time of Moses. In the spring, when the semi-nomadic shepherds would set out for new pasture grounds in preparation for the arrival of newborn sheep and goats, they would offer the gods the return of the first-born animal's life as a token of gratitude for, and as a plea for the safe arrival of, the anticipated many more to follow. The sacrifice culminates in the marking with the sacrificed victim's blood, which will ward off all dangers to them and to their animals, especially the young about to be born. The "destroyer" mentioned in Exodus 12:23 is the personification of all these threats to their safety.

In particular, it is this "blood rite" that enables the connection between their history and God's historic entry into it. When they are at their lowest ebb, and in greatest need of God's powerful outstretched arm, when the Pharaoh refuses to let up on them, God unleashes his ultimate weapon: the tenth and final plague. In Exodus 11:1 God tells Moses: "One more plague will I bring upon Pharaoh and upon Egypt. After that he will let you depart. In fact, he will not merely let you go; he will drive you away." Verse 4 says more: "At midnight I will go forth through Egypt. Every first-born in this land shall die, from the first-born of the Pharaoh on the throne to the first-born of the slave-girl at the handmill, as well as all the first-born of the animals." No wonder the Lord orders Moses, "Consecrate to me every first-born that opens the womb among the Israelites, both of man and beast, <u>for it belongs to me</u>" (Ex.13:1, emphasis added).

Later, in the book of Numbers (ch.3: 5-9, 12-13) we read: "The Lord said to Moses, 'Summon the tribe of Levi and present them to Aaron the priest, as his assistants. They shall discharge his obligations and those of the whole community before the meeting tent by serving at the Dwelling. You shall give the Levites to Aaron and his sons; they have been set aside from among the Israelites as dedicated to me. It is I who have chosen the Levites from the Israelites in place of every first-born that opens the womb among the Israelites. The Levites, therefore, are mine, because every first-born is mine. When I slew all the first-born in the land of Egypt, I made all the first-born in Israel sacred to me, both of man and of beast. They belong to me; I am the Lord.'"

In Exodus ch.12 the Lord tells Moses to order the people to ceremonially slaughter a year-old goat or lamb to roast and consume. "They shall take some of its blood and apply it to the two doorposts and the lintel of every house in which they partake of the lamb [v.7]. You are to eat it with your loins girt, sandals on your feet and your staff in hand, you shall eat like those who are in flight. It is the Passover of the Lord. For on this same night I will go through Egypt, striking down every first-born of the land, both man and beast, and executing judgment on all the gods of Egypt—I, the Lord! But the blood will mark the houses where you are. Seeing the blood, I will pass over you ...no destructive blow will come upon you [vv.11-13]."

By extending it into a new direction, they made this primitive, cultural gesture of seeking the safety of new pastures for new growth for themselves and their flocks, now point theologically to Israel's deliverance from the bondage of slavery to the freedom and safety of their own land—a gift from their gracious God, who has bonded himself to them and now, through Moses, asks them to observe this Passover "as a perpetual ordinance for yourselves and your descendants. You must observe this rite when you have entered the land which the Lord will give you as he promised. When your children ask you, 'What does this rite mean?' you shall reply, 'This is the Passover sacrifice of the Lord, who passed over the houses of the Israelites in Egypt, when he struck down the Egyptians, he spared our houses'" (Ex.12:24-27).

It's interesting that soon the Feast of the Passover, the hallmark of semi-nomadic wandering clans, is joined to the Feast of Unleavened Bread, the mark of a farming culture (what they'll become after occupying Canaan), celebrating the successful harvest of an agrarian, settled society. But it was a natural, since both feasts took place at about the same time of year, and both used the symbolism of bread with no time for leavening. In Exodus ch. 13 Moses says to the people: "Remember this day on which you came out of Egypt, that place of slavery. It was with a strong hand that the Lord brought you away. Nothing made with leaven must be eaten. For seven days you shall eat unleavened bread, and the seventh day shall also be a festival to the Lord. On this day you shall explain to your son, 'This is because of what the Lord did for me when I came out of Egypt.' Therefore, you shall keep this prescribed rite at its appointed time from year to year" (vv. 3, 6, 8, 10).

And isn't the point clear? God is the reason for the birth of their children, of their cattle, and of their crops. They will acknowledge their dependence on his bounty in the usual, primitive ways of their world, by making a (symbolic) return of the first-fruits. But they will infuse these ways with sophisticated theological insights, opening the way for Jesus' once-for-all, culminating sacrifice, foreshadowed at the Last Supper where he is both the saving lamb of sacrifice, in whose blood our sins are washed away, and the true bread from heaven come for the life of the world, so that our passing over is no longer from slavery to freedom, but from our world to his, from death to life!

Introduction

Celebrating the Lord's Supper with his friends on Holy Thursday night is the first step onto a bridge that will take us, with Jesus, from a sorrowful farewell to his brothers, all the way to a joyful "Welcome back!" from his Father. This feast we call simply "Holy Thursday" has been known by many other names, depending on the point of reference. Officially it is the <u>feria quinta in Coena Domini</u>, Thursday of the Lord's Supper, clearly commemorating the institution of the Holy Eucharist. It was also called <u>dies traditionis</u>, referring to the many <u>traditiones</u> (the Latin noun can mean a handing down, handing over, or a betrayal) that took place that day: after being betrayed by Judas, Jesus hands himself over to the arresting troops, and lastly, leaves us his body and blood in the Eucharist.

In German it is known as <u>Gruendonnerstag</u>, Thursday of weeping, referring to the final reconciliation of penitents that for many centuries took place on this day, following the public profession of guilt and repentance that lasted all through Lent. English Catholics have called it "Maundy Thursday," from the Latin rendering of Jesus' words: "<u>Mandatum novum do vobis</u>" (I give you a new commandment) when he orders us to imitate him in washing one another's feet as he did ours at his farewell supper, to the great astonishment of his disciples. But the most popular designation in the universal church remains simply Holy Thursday.

When Pope Pius XII revised the rites of Holy Week in 1955, he restored the time of the Holy Thursday Mass to the evening, in accord with the ancient custom of Jerusalem's Christians. There would be just the one evening Mass for each parish, with all the people and their ministers together, to make clear the oneness of this Eucharistic celebration. To further establish this night's uniqueness, the tabernacle is empty, so everyone becomes aware that they will receive the Holy Bread consecrated at this special Mass—the Lord gathers us together around himself, making us members of one family, at one table, sharing in the one banquet of his love.

The first reading (Exodus 12: 1-8, 11-14) provides the background and details for the Passover meal. The Hebrew people in Egypt are saved by the blood of the lamb daubed on their doors—God's wrath will "pass over" their homes. Once released by the Pharaoh they in turn will "pass over" from the land of slavery and death to the promised land of freedom and new life. The second reading (I Corinthians 11: 23-26) is the earliest written account of the Lord's Supper to circulate among the churches, thanks to Paul.

[Time out for brief chronological aside:
According to the Synoptics, Jesus was celebrating the Passover supper with this friends the night before he died (Luke 22:7-15; Matthew 26: 17-19; Mark 14: 12-17). With John, it's not that important whether or not Jesus' Last Supper was, in fact, the Passover meal. What counts for him is that Jesus dies at the same time that the Passover lambs were being slaughtered at

the temple—on the <u>eve</u> of Passover (John 19:14). The connection is stressed when he quotes (sounding, for once, very much like Matthew, "so that the scripture passage might be fulfilled") the Exodus 12: 46 requirement for the consumption of the lamb: "not a bone of it will be broken" (John 19:36) in depicting Jesus dying on the cross. And all this should remind us of how the evangelist had earlier described the encounter between the cousins at the Jordan, at the very threshold of Jesus' career, when he quotes the Baptist, on seeing Jesus coming toward him, "Behold, the Lamb of God, who takes away the sin of the world" (John 1:29).]

And it's interesting—no, it's downright surprising—that the gospel (John 13: 1-15) will feature not the glorious institution of the Eucharist but the humble washing of the feet: an obvious attempt by Jesus to point out to us the intimate, necessary connection between our worship of God and our service of one another. What's more, we don't just <u>hear</u> about the washing, we <u>see and experience</u> it when the presider, whose job/privilege it is to stand in for Jesus, removes his vestments, takes water and a towel and begins to wash the feet of twelve (what else?) members of the community. In the good old days they were twelve handpicked authority figures from the different parish groups: presidents of the Altar Society, of the Holy Name Society, etc. I've found it gratifying to see "ordinary" folk, members of the parish family being invited to come up. And even more so when the original "washees" kneel down to become washers of twelve others, who in turn…until the entire congregation has had the opportunity to participate in this humbling but uplifting experience of Jesus' new commandment of love for God expressed in mutual service.

It might seem out of place, at first glance, on this night when we gather around the table of the Lord to celebrate the institution of the Eucharist, and of the ordained priesthood, to find the washing of feet linked to the adoration of the Most Holy Sacrament. But if we think about it, we might just find it a very meaningful combination. Because if your plan is to thank Jesus for the gift of the Eucharist, to adore his enduring presence in the Sacrament of the Altar, this liturgy will force you to go beyond: the presence of Christ in the Eucharist is not an end in itself, but the means to building up the community into the Body of Christ, his living presence here and now. It isn't enough to ask God to send his Holy Spirit upon the gifts of bread and wine so that they may become for us the Body and Blood of Christ, without calling down the Holy Spirit also upon the community, so that "we who are nourished by his Body and Blood may become one body, one spirit, in Christ," as we pray in the Eucharistic Prayer III.

It's easier on us to see Christ in the Blessed Sacrament than to discern him in the faces of the ordinary men and women around us at the Lord's table. And now, in the midst of solemnly recalling the institution of the Eucharist and the incomprehensible miracle of God's continuing presence among us...we wash each other's feet! It doesn't get any more "ordinary" than that: simple, loving service for our brothers and sisters in the building up of the one Body of Christ. Just as the Passover meal became for the Jews a memorial that not only called to mind the Exodus experience but made it somehow present to them (and they to it), so does this humble service to others, along with the breaking of the bread and the partaking of the cup, now make present to us the great saving act of Jesus on the cross.

Since there will be no Mass on Good Friday, we end tonight's liturgy by taking the Eucharist which will be shared tomorrow— a clear sign of the continuum between the two feasts—in procession to a tabernacle prepared for it, where it will be venerated overnight. At this temporary Altar of Repose the consecrated hosts are reserved till Good Friday's Communion service, though the veneration of the Blessed Sacrament (keeping watch with Jesus as he prayed in the Garden, remember?) is prescribed only until midnight. Once the procession leaves the church, we set the stage for Friday's liturgy. The altar is stripped, to the words of the antiphon "They divided my garments among them," an allusion to the treatment of Christ before they crucified him.

This procession with the reserved Sacrament to the place of repose is about the only present-day instance of a practice that had been common in the church's past: setting aside consecrated Hosts for the sick, and for Holy Communion on days when the Eucharist was not celebrated. Originally there was no special ceremony involved—as soon as Mass was over the deacon took the consecrated Hosts in the pyx (often dove-shaped, sometimes hung in a hovering position over the altar) from the main altar to the sacristy, where they were reserved until needed for distribution to the faithful.

During the Middle Ages this altogether practical procedure morphed into an elaborate ritual, with the first mention of a formal procession coming in the 11th century. Quite naturally, once Good Friday became the one day of the year without a Mass, reserving the Eucharist for Communion acquired even greater ceremony. Medieval preachers were a hit with allegories, the practice of discovering (maybe even planting) a hidden special meaning to each and every detail of gospel stories or church ceremonies. More than likely an ingenious procedure for an unlettered audience who could visualize but not read up on details. For example, the placing of the Blessed Sacrament in a special repository made them think of the burial of Christ. In fact, in some places the repository came to be called a sepulchrum.

There was a decline in the reception of Communion by the faithful on Good Friday, as well as in general. In reaction to doctrinal attacks by dissenting Christians from the Reformation onwards, the church hugely emphasized the real presence of the all-holy, divine Jesus in the Host, to such a degree that many of the laity were afraid to approach and receive, considering themselves unworthy of physical contact with such great holiness. To look upon the consecrated Host in the monstrance (from a safe distance) and receive the blessing at the end of Benediction was becoming the vastly more popular "contact point" of the lay peo-

ple and their Savior, but what a far cry from Jesus' "take and eat."
(The priest, of course, was ordained for his job, so no problem.)

This development contributed to the medieval symbolism, since it
was now necessary to reserve only one large Host, for the
celebrant. This was easily done in a chalice, instead of in the pyx
formerly used for the congregation to receive, and the chalice was
in turn covered with a corporal, which would be seen as a
symbol of the shroud that wrapped our Lord in his tomb. Then
there developed the custom of holding a night-long watch at this
repository, as though at the tomb of Christ. Church historians
discover in this practice the remote beginnings of the Forty Hours'
devotion, fusing two distinct devotions into one: veneration of the
reserved Sacrament, and a pious watch at the tomb of Christ.

The reform of 1955 finally simplified (read: cleaned up) the practice
of the repository, not in order to discourage devotion in any way,
but to de-emphasize what is really only secondary to the main
events celebrated in the Triduum. The repository does not symbol-
ize the tomb of Christ, and the object of Holy Thursday and
Good Friday is not the adoration of the Eucharist (basically static),
but the celebration of the whole Paschal mystery (the ongoing
process that continues into the Vigil). The true idea behind the
watch kept before the repository is that we have a chance to
do what the Apostles failed to do—keep watch with Christ
throughout his agony in the garden.

[An aside on Holy Thursday's Chrism Mass:

Pius XII's revised Order of Holy Week called for a special Mass of Chrism, distinct from the solemn evening liturgy, to be celebrated in the morning at each Bishop's cathedral. He gathers all his priests and consecrates the holy oils which will be needed for the blessing of the baptismal water and for the confirming of the catechumens at the Easter Vigil—this is the last day available for that consecration, since it will be the last Mass celebrated before the Vigil. Over the years, many bishops have opted to move the Chrism Mass forward, so as to preserve the unifying impact of just the one Mass on Holy Thursday night.]

Mass of the Lord's Supper

Scripture and Reflections

Exodus 12: 1-8, 11-14 *The Lord said to Moses, "Tell the whole community of Israel: On the tenth of this month every one of your families must procure for itself a lamb, a year-old male without blemish, either from the sheep or the goats. It shall be slaughtered during the evening twilight. They shall take some of its blood and apply it to the two doorposts and the lintel of every house in which they partake of the lamb. This is how you are to eat it: with your loins girt, sandals on your feet and your staff in hand, like those who are in flight. It is the Passover of the Lord. For on this same night I will go through Egypt, striking down every first-born of the land, both man and beast, and executing judgment on all the gods of Egypt—I, the Lord! But the blood will mark the houses where you are. Seeing* *the blood, I will pass over you. This day shall be a memorial feast for you, as a perpetual institution."*

Responsorial Psalm 116: 12-13, 15-16, 17-18

I Corinthians 11: 23-26 *The Lord Jesus, on the night in which he was betrayed, took bread and after he had given thanks, broke it and said, "This is my body, which is for you. Do this in remembrance of me." In the same way, after the supper, he took the cup, saying, "This cup is the new covenant in my blood. Do this, whenever you drink it, in remembrance of me." Every time, then, you eat this bread and drink this cup, you proclaim the death of the Lord until he comes!*

John 13: 1-15 *Before the feast of Passover, Jesus realized that the hour had come for him to pass from this world to the Father. [He] rose from the meal and took off his cloak. He picked up a towel and tied it around himself. Then he poured water into a basin and began to wash his disciples' feet and dry them with the towel. After he had washed their feet he put his cloak back on and reclined at table once more. He said to them: "Do you understand what I just did for you? You address me as 'Teacher' and 'Lord,' and fittingly enough, for that is what I am. But if I washed your feet—I who am Teacher and Lord—then you must wash each other's feet. What I just did was to give you an example: as I have done, so you must do."*

Reflection:

By his blood we are saved. We wash away the stain of our sins in the blood of the Lamb. Jesus takes our sins with him onto that cross, and when he dies, they die with him, giving us a clean slate, a new beginning, a reason for grateful hope. This Passover business describes beautifully, albeit painfully, our escape from the sanctions of the law into the wonders of the freedom of God's children. This is what Jesus is celebrating with his friends as they share in the Passover meal on that last Thursday night before his death. The apostles were recalling the Israelites' exodus from Egypt to the Promised Land. Jesus has in mind <u>our</u> exodus from this passing world into never-ending life with him and the Father, linked together in and by the Holy Spirit. It becomes for them, and remains for us, a "perpetual institution," a memorial that not only depicts but also makes present the sacred event it recalls. Jesus doesn't die over and over—this memorial allows us to enter into the saving mystery of his once-for-all death.

The paradox of the cross as a life-giving instrument of death is pre-figured in this topsy-turvy image of leadership. The master does not demand the service that is rightfully his due. Instead, he teach-es—in action first, then in words—that a Christian leads others by serving them, not bossing them. The only way others can truly live is if we die to ourselves and give <u>them</u> the space, the spotlight, the attention they require. These little, painful, constant deaths pre-pare us for the final taking leave of ourselves in answer to God's call. "Take up your cross daily...."

Three
TRIDUUM – GOOD FRIDAY

Introduction

From very early in the church's history Good Friday was known as the Pasch of the Crucifixion, with Easter being called the Pasch of the Resurrection. The mystery of the cross overshadows the entire Good Friday liturgy: an instrument of ignominy and death that becomes a sign of life and glory. During the Middle Ages, all these services had been getting pushed into earlier starts, ending up as morning services. (Imagine the Easter Vigil's blessing the new fire, for example, in the late morning light instead of in the darkness of night, or singing the Exsultet next to the Paschal Candle in broad daylight.) The people's devotion filled the resulting void on Good Friday with the Tre Ore (Italian: three hours) and/or the Way of the Cross—heartfelt accompaniments to honor the Lord's final hours on the cross. (When Pius XII returned to the original custom, he made the service begin between 3 and 8 p.m.)

Good Friday's liturgy is solemn but not funereal, not an occasion for mourning or sorrow, but rather for fasting and prayer and reflection that considers as one inclusive, continuous event the Lord's dying-and-rising. The readings tell of a servant who, though suffering, sees the light of the fullness of days, of a people with a high priest who, obedient unto death, becomes the source of life for his followers, of a chosen race whose king reigns from a cross.

The church observes a special fast now, different from our Lenten fasting. The Constitution on the Sacred Liturgy recommends that the paschal fast be observed everywhere on Good Friday and, where possible, on Holy Saturday. The whole church fasts, those already baptized accompanying those who are to be baptized tomorrow night. This fast is how the catechumens prepare for their baptism, and how their welcoming family expresses its solidarity with them.

Because it is in a continuum, Good Friday is also Easter: we celebrate the risen Lord. And so the church sets up the veneration, not of the crucifix (with Jesus' body nailed on it), but of the cross. "Christ has died. Christ is risen. Christ will [on the last day] come again." The altar is bare, without cloths or candles. There is no Mass—in accordance with the church's ancient tradition the sacraments are not celebrated today or tomorrow. There are no greetings, no genuflections, no opening songs or processions.

The unbroken flow between these days is obvious: there was no dismissal at the end of Mass last night, and there is no official start to today's ceremonies. We simply assemble and prostrate ourselves in humble submission before the word and the glorious cross of Christ.

The first reading is from Isaiah (52:13 - 53:12), the fourth and final servant song, presenting one who suffers in order to expiate the sins of the people—crushed for our sins, he will still receive a place of honor among the great, because God will vindicate him. But how can a crucifixion have any glory to it? The paradox appears again in the second reading (Hebrews 4:14-16 and 5:7-9) which speaks of a high priest who, Son though he was, learned obedience from what he suffered! The cross taught Jesus something? Did we hear right?

This paradox cannot be explained; it can only be experienced, and that experience is what John's account of the passion of Jesus offers his readers. His version of the story is very different from what we heard on Palm Sunday. Here, Jesus is not a victim; he's in control of everything that happens. For example, there is no reference to any reluctance in Jesus' prayer at the garden. Faced with impending suffering, persecution, and even death, Jesus says simply: "Now is my soul troubled. And what shall I say—Father, save me from his hour? No, for this purpose I have come to this hour. Father, glorify thy name" (12:27-28a). "I'm ready, let's get started."

When the arresting officers arrive (18:1-27) there's no need for Judas to identify him with a kiss. Jesus, "knowing all that was to befall him" (v.4), takes the initiative, steps forward, and asks them "Whom do you seek?" When they answer, he identifies himself with the unequivocal "I am he" (v.6). This is such an explicit claim to Lordship that it bowls over his accusers—literally—they fall to the ground. (If you think I'm exaggerating, check it out: it's in the Book.) Remember how John's Jesus makes repeated and clear connections between himself and Yahweh ("I am who am") in all his "I am" statements? (I am the Bread of Life. I am the Good Shepherd. I am the way, and the truth, and the life. I am the true Bread from Heaven. I am the gate. I am the resurrection. Etc. Now back to our story.) What would you do if the people who came to take you away ended up on the ground? Not Jesus. He gives them another chance to get it right, and asks them again, "Whom do you seek?" "C'mon, let's get on with it!"

Not surprisingly, in this telling of the story of his passion and death, Jesus needs no help to carry his cross, he can carry it himself, thank you. There is no cry of abandonment, "Why have you forsaken me?" because in 16:32 John quotes Jesus: "I am not alone, because the Father is with me." "The Father loves me because I lay down my life. No one takes it from me; I lay it down of my own free will, and as it is in my power to lay it down, so it is in my power to take it up again" (10:17-18). The cross does not defeat him, he makes it his throne, and reigns in glory from it. So the cross becomes our glory; the instrument of his death has become the instrument of our salvation.

After proclaiming the Passion of the Lord we join the church in her most solemn and clearly universal version of the General Intercessions, and ask that the redeeming death of Christ reach into the lives of all men and women, into the whole world. Now only two ceremonies remain: a simple Communion service dispensing the Eucharist reserved from last night's Mass, and a rite fittingly unique to this day—the veneration of a large cross.

In awe over the tremendous events of Good Friday, the church had no celebration of any kind on this day, so naturally no one received Communion. And yet, since we best commemorate the Passion by receiving the memoria Passionis, the memorial of the Passion, no other ritual could unite us so closely to the sacrificed Christ as the reception of Communion on this special day. Eventually the church recognized and promoted this devotion, but not until the 8th century did the Roman Ritual even mention it. Besides, an overzealous, if well-intended, stress on the divinity and sublime holiness of Jesus really and truly present in the Host backfired, resulting in a decreasing participation in Communion.

Ever hear old-timers wonder how you can go to Communion so blithely, since you haven't been to confession (meaning the night before)? Most lay people just watched as the priest received. (The ringing of bells to focus attention on the special moment of consecration, with the subsequent elevation so the people behind the priest could see the sacred elements, dates from the same time and same frame of mind. People felt unworthy of receiving, so they made a special point of watching, for example at

Benediction, or going from altar to altar, or even from church to church, to "catch" as many consecration/elevations as they could. What a shame—all that devotion misplaced....) At first the people just stayed away; eventually they would be <u>forbidden</u> to receive on Good Friday. This prohibition had to be repeated several times during the 17th century, which means that at least in some places some people continued to receive. Not long after, thank God, we returned to our earlier ways.

Another medieval development resulted in making this simple service into what would come to be called the "Mass of the Presanctified," by the addition of ceremonies to give the service the appearance of a real Mass, everything <u>minus</u> the consecration. Pius XII ended this by restoring the original communion service, with this significant difference: Communion would not be distributed in silence as it once was, but accompanied by singing. Liturgically the Eucharist is a social sacrament, requiring a corporate setting, a family gathered around a table, and nothing unites us in common celebration as joining in song.

Finally, while the church does not "proclaim the death of the Lord" sacramentally on this day, it does so in another way: by the rite of the veneration of the cross. This is one of the oldest of Good Friday observances, though not in its present form. It began, like so many other Holy Week customs, in the popular devotion of Jerusalem's Christians. By the 4th century they would gather at Golgotha on the morning of Good Friday, with their bishop seated between his deacons at a linen-covered table with a relic of the true cross placed on it. He held the ends of the cross containing the relic in his hands, and then the catechumens and all the faithful would come close to venerate it, all in a reverential and complete silence.

As pilgrims would return home, other churches began to follow suit, especially those fortunate enough to have access to a relic of the true cross. (The others would just use a plain wooden cross.) We understand the veneration rite only if we remember that it was originally directed to (a relic of) the true cross itself. Our earliest record of its use in the Good Friday services in Rome is from the 8th century. Starting from his own basilica, the Church of St. John Lateran, the Pope and his retinue process to the nearby Church of the Holy Cross, with the relic of the true cross and the Pope walking barefoot before it, with a smoking censer. Once there, subdeacons offer the relic for the people's veneration also. Psalms and hymns are added for accompaniment, and eventually the <u>Ecce, lignum crucis</u> ("Behold the wood of the cross") is sung while the cross is shown, by unveiling, to all.

[A historical aside: There was a time (which some of us can remember, I'm sure) when, starting on Sunday before Palm Sunday, the church provided a Lent-for-the-eyes by covering all its interior statues and crucifixes with a purple cloth. As a kid in Caracas, Venezuela, I remember being quite taken by the dramatic change as I entered church and saw large purple "bags" all around me, covering all the statues. They stayed on for almost two weeks, until the singing of this hymn on Good Friday, with the celebrant carrying the veiled crucifix up the center aisle and marking three pauses, each time unveiling part of the crucifix (one arm, then also the head, and finally all of it) while intoning, in progressively higher tones, this famous antiphon "<u>Ecce, lignum crucis</u>," with the assembly singing it reverently after him. Not only that, there was a matching Lent-for-the-ears which forbade the use of the bells in church, from the joyful <u>Gloria</u> of Holy Thursday's Mass till the triumphant <u>Gloria</u> of the Easter Vigil Service. Tintinnabulation was considered too joyful for this time, so in many places, blocks of wood replaced the bells, so you'd hear a dull "thwack" to announce the consecration.]

In our contemporary revision, a large cross is presented to the congregation, so that we can approach this instrument of cruel torture and shameful death, to reverence it with a touch or a kiss! We've become so used to this symbol—imagine if we were asked to kiss an electric chair, or a 13-looped noose? That's the impact the cross must have had on early Christians: a startling paradox to accept and appreciate in faith.

Four Accounts of the Passion and Death of our Lord

Given the distinct situations of the four evangelists, we should not be surprised that their portraits of the Lord are dissimilar. Mark's is the oldest gospel, the pioneer in this genre. His Jesus is an itinerant preacher, in a hurry to get out to as many places as he can to announce the Good News of God's arriving Kingdom. Mark reports more what Jesus <u>did</u> than what he <u>said</u>. Matthew is in great contrast on the organizing of Jesus' words into teaching packets, so to speak, which made his gospel a favorite for the early church's instructing of new converts into the mind and the ways of Jesus. Luke, like Matthew before him, will borrow heavily from Mark's material, but also pointedly select the episodes of Jesus' life that are healing, forgiving, and reach out to women, to sinners and outsiders.

Because they obviously share so much material, and are written probably within 15 years of each other, they are called the "Synoptic Gospels," from the Greek <u>syn optein</u>, meaning to see together, or alike. John's gospel will come from many years later, and from a quite original point of view. His Jesus, while not losing any of his humanity, is clearly one with God. He is never harried by crowds—his discourses are with individuals, usually. He is majestic, divine, always in control.

Other differences will appear candidly in the telling of Jesus' passion and death in each gospel. Mark, in chapters 14+15, presents a stark human abandonment of the Lord which dramatically reverses at the end, but only at the very end. From the moment Jesus goes to the Mount of Olives—in agony over his impending death—the behavior of his disciples is portrayed negatively. While he prays, they fall asleep—three times! Judas betrays him. Peter (the Rock?) repeatedly denies him. All his friends flee, the last one leaving his clothes behind (in the grasp of his questioner) as he tears away from Jesus—just the opposite of leaving all things to <u>follow</u> him! Jesus' only word from the cross is "My God, my God, why have you forsaken me?" And yet...as Jesus breathes his last, God acts to confirm his Son: the Temple veil is rent, and the Roman centurion (testifying in place of the AWOL disciples) declares, "Truly this was God's son." So, after all his suffering, Jesus is vindicated by a faithful God.

Matthew's chapters 26+27 echo Mark closely, adding his hallmark "and-this-happened-in-order-to-fulfill" pointers, so that his Jewish-convert audience can see how Jesus really was the promised Messiah, the fulfillment of all those Old Testament promises they anchored their hopes on. Luke's version of the Passion (chapters 22+23) depicts the disciplines in a much more sympathetic light, for they have remained faithful to Jesus in his trials. At Gethsemane they fall asleep once (not three times), and it's on account of their heavy sorrow. Jesus, for his part, seems to be less anguished by his own fate than by his ubiquitous concern for others: he heals the slave's ear at his arrest; on the way to Calvary he worries about the fate of the women; he forgives those who crucify him; he promises Paradise to the penitent thief. The crucifixion has become the occasion of divine forgiveness and care. Finally, Jesus dies peacefully, praying, "Father, into your hands I commit my spirit."

John's chapters 18+19 present a sovereign Jesus who has defiantly announced, "I lay down my life and I take it up again; no one takes it from me" (10:17-18). Pilate is afraid before the Son of God who tells him flat out, "You have no power over me." Jesus is not a victim; in fact, he's in control. At Gethsemane, as we have seen, the specter of his doom barely gives him pause—he's eager to meet his fate. Also in marked contrast to the Synoptics, Jesus is not alone on Calvary. At the foot of the cross we find his mother and the beloved disciple, whom he joins into a family of believing disciples that he leaves as his legacy. He does not cry out, "My God, why have you forsaken me?" because he has already assured us (16:32) that the Father is always with him. And his final word, in keeping with the control he's had all along, is a decision to hand over his spirit, now that "It is finished." And even death can't stop him: to prove that he's dead the soldier will pierce his heart with a lance, and out comes blood—and water! The "living water" he had promised the Samaritan woman at the well: "whoever drinks the water I shall give will never thirst; the water I shall give will become in him a spring of water welling up to eternal life" (10:14). As his heart stops, our life starts: the water of Baptism and the blood of the Eucharist.

When these different Passion narratives are read one by one, we should not be upset by the contrasting accounts, nor wonder which is the "correct" picture of what "actually happened." All four are given to us by the inspiration of the Spirit, and no single one of them exhausts the meaning of Jesus, which is what each evangelist hoped to bring to us.

Commemoration of Our Lord's Passion and Death

Scripture and Reflections

Isaiah 52:13 – 53:12 *My servant shall be raised high and greatly exalted. / There was in him no stately bearing to make us look at him, nor appearance that would attract us to him. / He was spurned and avoided by men, a man of suffering, accustomed to infirmity, / one of those from whom men hide their faces, spurned, and we held him in no esteem. / Yet it was our infirmities that he bore, our sufferings that he endured. / He was pierced for our offenses, crushed for our sins; / by his stripes we were healed. / The Lord laid upon him the guilt of us all. / Though he was harshly treated, he submitted and opened not his mouth; / like a lamb led to the slaughter or a sheep before the shearers, he was silent and opened not his mouth. / A grave was assigned him among the wicked and a burial place with evildoers, / though he had done no wrong nor spoken any falsehood. / But the will of the Lord will be accomplished through him. / Through his suffering, my servant shall justify many, and their guilt he shall bear. / And he shall take away the sins of many, and win pardon for their offenses.*

Responsorial Psalm 31: 2, 6, 12-13, 15-16, 17, 25 *In you, O Lord, I take refuge; let me never be put to shame. In your justice rescue me. Into your hands I commend my spirit; you will redeem me, O Lord, O faithful God. I am an object of reproach; I am like a dish that is broken. But my trust is in you, O Lord; I say "You are my God." In your hands is my destiny; rescue me; save me in your kindness. Take courage and be stouthearted, all you who hope in the Lord.*

Hebrews 4: 14-16; 5: 7-9 *We have a great high priest who has passed through the heavens, Jesus, the Son of God; not a high priest who is unable to sympathize with our weakness, but one who was tempted in every way that we are, yet never sinned. So let us confidently approach the throne of grace to receive mercy and favor and to find help in time of need. Son though he was [Christ] learned obedience from what he suffered; and when perfected, he became the source of eternal salvation for all who obey him.*

John 18:1 – 19: 42 (We trust you understand that any attempt to condense, or even to paraphrase this powerful account would leave us missing out/wanting more. Thanks.)

Reflection:

This is rightly the most famous of the four "Servant Songs" of Second Isaiah, an uncanny description of Jesus, God's chosen servant, who will freely and willingly take on all our ills in order to render us fit for his undeserved and unbelievable call to become his brothers and sisters, thus entitled and even encouraged to call Yahweh our Abba! What a noble gesture! And it's not just a gesture, either. When he is scourged, each time an angry welt is left on his back, the nasty scars of our sins disappear from ours! When we stop and consider this image, when we picture it, we are rightly dismayed at the insufficiency of our gratitude—if we show it only in words. This calls for us to join our pains and suffer-ings to his, to offer for the good of others any absorbing of evil we can carry out, returning blessings for curses, quiet acceptance for vile words/actions directed at us, peace in return for violence.

What could the author of <u>Hebrews</u> have in mind when he claims Jesus learned, in fact, became perfected, by submitting to suffering? I imagine what he gained in obedience to the Father was the <u>experience</u> of total powerlessness leading to total exaltation. Because he emptied himself so completely, accepting death, death on a cross, he was able to be filled totally by the Father's gift of Spirit/Risen Life before dawn on Easter morning. This is the intimacy with God he offers each of us. It's only our reluctance to step aside, to make room, that limits God's full entry into our lives.

(Reflections on the gospel selection have appeared above in the Introduction and in the discussion of the four Passion accounts.)

Four

TRIDUUM – HOLY SATURDAY NIGHT

Introduction

Holy Saturday (the day) has been from the beginning devoted to observing and accompanying the Lord's Sabbath rest in his tomb. In the early church, the day was spent in rest, in prayer, in quiet and collected expectation of the Resurrection, and in a strict fast—yes, Saturday too. The Easter Vigil, as the Holy Saturday Night service is properly known, is not a preparation for Easter. Nor is it, in the usual sense of our Saturday night celebration of the Vigil of Sunday, an anticipatory celebration of the next day's feast. The Easter Vigil is the <u>true</u> celebration of Easter itself. St. Augustine calls it "the mother of all vigils," meaning this is the most important night-watch of the whole liturgical year. The reason Pius XII restored the Vigil to its proper place—at night, not pushed earlier into the day—was so as to emphasize a truth that had become obscured (by occurring in the light): the Vigil is the Easter feast. The Lord is raised from the tomb during the night, before the first light of Sunday morning's dawn reveals his absence to his followers. How fitting that the sublime mystery of this event is veiled by the darkness of night.

We do well to look to the dictionary definition of vigil, "a purposeful or watchful staying awake during the ordinary hours of sleep." We wait and watch—remember Jesus asking (in vain) for his friends to stay awake and lend him moral support while he went off to pray nearby? We wait with the catechumens preparing for their release from sin and entry into a new life. As the watchman waits for the dawn, so my soul waits for the Lord…. No wonder St. Augustine called this night "the mother of all vigils."

Whereas Jerusalem and the Eastern churches always observed this chronology, Rome and the churches of the West kept anticipating the time little by little, so that by 1570 it was celebrated in the early hours of the morning, almost a full day ahead of schedule, where it stayed, thanks to the iron-clad regulations of the revised Missal of Pius V, until Pius XII in 1951 returned it to its original time. Until this reform, the feast had lost any meaningful observance of quiet, reverential time to accompany the Lord's Sabbath, while at the same time losing the powerful symbolism of light breaking in on darkness. The night setting is not for sentimental reasons—it is integral to the event it celebrates, so much so that today we are forbidden to begin the celebration until the onset of darkness.

The Jewish Passover, which Christ was commemorating with his disciples at his farewell supper, took place at night, a night on which the Lord God himself keeps vigil, until "at midnight" he goes out throughout the land to slay every first-born and speed the release of his people by the Pharaoh (Exodus 12:29). The Jews, in fact, see themselves as being formed into his people on this night, taken by the hand, set aside for their passing to their new freedom, consecrated for God by his choice. Just so the Church, the New Israel, is called into being as the Body of Christ on this night, when Christ takes up his glorious, risen life. This is why we celebrate Baptisms on this night, because this is the sacrament of our being born into the Church, the People of God. Remember Romans 6? "Through baptism into his death we were buried with him...if we have died with Christ, we believe that we are also to live with him" (vv. 4, 8).

Four Elements of the Easter Vigil

I. The Service of Light

For us, Easter comes in spring. The Lord's rising from the tomb to new life coincides with the earth's return from the dead of winter to the sprouting of spring. The long nights and short days, with the sun's invigorating intensity dimmed and abbreviated, now begin to give way to shorter nights with longer days that bring us more of the sun's heat and life-promoting power. Night gives way to day; darkness is overcome by light. In Christian terms, we pass over, from the death/darkness of sin to the new life/light of God's glory in Christ, "who called you out of darkness into his wonderful light" (1 Peter 2:9).

Blessing of the New Fire

These introductory ceremonies prepare us for the Vigil, so it's appropriate that they take place, not inside the church, but in the darkness outside, before we come in. In today's world of handy tools, a long-necked gas-fueled candle lighter produces a flame with a flick of a Bic, so to speak. But the church recalls the ancient, cumbersome method of starting a fire from the spark of a flint-stone. It's not the technique—it's the symbolism: as fire begins from a spark struck from a stone, so our light comes from the risen Christ, "the stone [once] rejected by the builders," which now "has become the cornerstone" (Psalm 118:22 quoted by Jesus in Matthew 21:42 and Luke 20:17). And the whole point of the new fire is that from it will be lit the paschal candle, the symbol of Christ breaking through death to new life. They thought they had snuffed him out, but like those trick candles on birthday cakes, his flame just wouldn't go out!

Paschal Candle

From this new fire, stuck from Christ, the loyal and suffering servant who set his face like flint, comes the lighting of the Easter candle, the pre-eminent symbol of the risen Christ, victorious over death, triumphant over sin and darkness. One of the happiest changes introduced by Pius XII, and it was more a return to the early church's ways than an innovation, is to have the Paschal candle blessed and lit outside, before the service, and then have it (Christ, at the head of his body, the assembled believers) lead the procession into the church. (Prior to 1955 this rite took place inside the church, and then not till halfway through the singing of the Easter acclamation, the Exsultet.)

The Paschal candle is clearly the focus of our attention. Its dimensions make it stand out; it is carried not by altar servers but by the deacon. It is marked by the celebrant with the symbolic monogram of Christ, the XP (chi rho, the first two letters of his name in Greek, pronounced: Cairo, as in Egypt). With a stylus he traces the cross and then inserts five red grains of incense to represent Christ's five wounds, adds the Alpha and the Omega and the year. So there you have it: Christ is with us tonight, in our time, leading us out of the darkness into God's light. We see it happen as the deacon carries this sturdy candle, with its thick wick and steady light, into the darkened church. (In those simpler times, there was no fire marshal with requirements for EXIT lights in the dark—it was flat out dark.) The procession vividly dramatized the effect of Christ's resurrection. When the deacon stops and sings out "Christ our Light!" the assembly responds with a glad "Thanks be to God!" Three times the procession pauses for this chanted exchange, and each time the faithful light their little hand-held candles from the King-sized Paschal candle as it marches up the church passing through their midst, and in doing so, they lay claim to their share in the glory of Christ's resurrection. We have been enlightened by Christ; we are sent to bring his light to others, to be the light of the world.

[On this occasion, some forty years ago, when I was a student of theology at the Old Mission in Santa Barbara, California, I had a wonderful epiphany. I was singing in the choir, so from the choir loft was able to see the effect of one strong candle stopping to share its light with a rippling circle of little candles, till the whole church was filled with faces all aglow. It was beautiful, looking down from high above and seeing that church full of darkness become a warm, resplendent "veritable sea of faces," as they say. I can honestly say I was genuinely sorry to see the electric lights come on as the celebration progressed.]

When he reaches the sanctuary, the deacon plants the Paschal candle firmly on its elevated base, and stands beside it to sing (and this really is an exultant Gregorian chant) "Exsultet iam angelica turba caelorum" "Let the heavenly crowd of angels exult" in honor of the Paschal candle and the crucified-and-risen, seemingly-defeated-but-ultimately-victorious Jesus it represents. Through the sacred mysteries of Baptism, Confirmation, and the Eucharist (soon to be celebrated) Jesus leads us, incorporates us, into his

Passover from life on earth as one with us...to life in heaven as one with the Father!

II. The Liturgy of the Word

Introduction

Around the fire we gather and keep watch and tell our story, recounting our history, the Heilsgeschichte (salvation history) of our people, all the way back from the forming of our tribes into a people, unified by our common alliance with God, or rather, by God's covenant with us. We marvel at, and glory in, the great moments of God's saving actions on our behalf throughout our history: creation, Abraham's sacrifice, God's mighty power in the Exodus, the passing through the Red Sea; just the way the Pilgrims might have gathered around a campfire to retell the stories of how they survived the religious persecutions in their villages back in England, and how they made it across the dangerous waters to this new land of freedom and, with hard work and God's help, plenty; or the way we gather at the table of our family elders, to enjoy hearing again how grandpa met grandma, and of their struggles to make a home for themselves after setting out on their own—with the telling becoming even more precious and meaningful after they are gone, and we have only these memories of them. This is family story time, going back as far as we can remember from what was handed down to us.

Scripture and Reflections

<u>First Reading</u>

Genesis 1:1 – 2:2   The reading takes us back in our history, back as far as we can go, back to the moment when it all started. *In the beginning, when God created the heavens and the earth, the earth was a formless wasteland, and darkness covered the abyss, while a mighty wind swept over the waters.*   God separated the darkness (night) from the light (day) and there you have it: *Thus evening came, and morning followed—the first day.*   On the second day he separated the waters above from those below, and called the dome "the sky." Next day he gathered the waters below into its basin (the sea), so that dry land appeared (earth).   *God saw how good it wa*s, and he made the earth bring forth vegetation.   On the fourth day *God made the two great lights, the greater one to govern the day, and the lesser one to govern the night, and he made the stars.*   And again he saw how good it was.   The next day he filled the skies with birds and the seas with swimming creatures, and saw how good it was. Finally, on the sixth day, he said, *Let the earth bring forth all kinds of living creatures: cattle, creeping things, and wild animals of all kinds. God saw how good it was. Then God said: "Let us make man in our image, after our likeness"…male and female he created them.* Then he blessed them, and gave them dominion over all living things he had created.   *God looked at everything he had made, and he found it very good.*   And since on the seventh day God was finished with all his work, he rested.

Reflection:

That mighty "wind" is rendered <u>ruah</u> in Hebrew, <u>pneuma</u> in Greek, and <u>spiritus</u> in Latin. It can also refer to spirit and to breath (pneumonia, anyone?), as in to inspire/breathe in, or expire/breathe out, or more dramatically, to breathe out and no longer in, meaning you die/expire. So this is God's life-giving breath, the Holy Spirit, that we Christians see at work in the creation of all things living...from God's own life. (Remember the sound of a mighty wind rushing about the upper room at Pentecost, the sound of the Holy Spirit's power-filled arrival, bringing the dispirited group back to life?)

It's noteworthy how much pleasure God takes in his handiwork as he goes along, like a carpenter who sizes up a piece of wood, notes its grain, shapes it carefully, sands it down, applies a varnish—admiring it every step of the way, until he finds it very good when he's all finished. Another point to note: at the time of this writing the Israelites' pagan neighbors vigorously promoted a cult of the sun and the moon, so the writer won't even use their names, just calling them the greater and lesser lights! And making sure to credit Yahweh for their origin.... The final touch, having God observe the Sabbath rest, is a stroke of (inspired) genius: how can we not keep this day holy if God himself sets the pace?

Second Reading

Genesis 22:1-18 *God put Abraham to the test, and said: "Take your son Isaac, your only one, whom you love, and offer him up as a* *holocaust on a height I will point out to you." On the third day Abraham got sight of the place from afar, [and] said to his servants: "Both of you stay here with the donkey, while the boy and I go over yonder. We will worship and then come back to you." Abraham took the wood for the holocaust and laid it on his son Isaac's shoulders, while he himself carried the fire and the knife. As the two walked on together, Isaac spoke to his father: "Here are the fire and the wood, but where is the sheep for the holocaust?" "Son," Abraham answered, "God himself will provide [it]." Abraham built an altar and arranged the wood on it. Next he tied up his son Isaac and put him on top of the wood. Then he reached out and took the knife to slaughter his son. But the Lord's messenger called to him from heaven, "Abraham, Abraham! Do not lay your hand on the boy. I know now how devoted you are to God, since you did not withhold from me your own beloved son." As Abraham looked about, he spied a ram caught by its horns in the thicket. So he took the ram and offered it up as a holocaust in place of his son. Again the Lord's messenger said: "I swear by myself, declares the Lord, that because you acted as you did in not withholding from me your beloved son, I will bless you abundantly and make your descendants as countless as the stars of the sky and the sands of the seashore; and in your descendants all the nations of the earth shall find blessing—all this because you obeyed my command."*

Reflection:

"On the third day" Abraham caught sight of the place...how long those days must have been for him! He shared his burden with no one, so it must have filled his mind and heart. This was the promised child from his beloved Sarah, the son who would begin a torrent of life to follow! But Yahweh wanted him back: talk about "the Lord giveth, the Lord taketh away...." The poignancy—and the heartbreak—of the child's innocent question: so where's the sacrificial lamb? Remember the first thing out of John the Baptist's mouth when he spotted his cousin Jesus coming toward him? "Behold the Lamb of God, who takes away the sin of the world" (John 1:29). Here, God can't bring himself to allow Abraham to go through with the sacrifice—his willingness will suffice, and yet, when it comes to <u>his</u> own Son, God will simply ask Jesus to do whatever it takes to show us how much we are loved by our Father, and then will watch his Son accept death, death on a cross, on our behalf.

Third Reading

Exodus 14:15 – 15:1 *The Lord said to Moses, "Lift up your staff and, with hand outstretched over the sea, split the sea in two, that the Israelites may pass through it on dry land. I will make the Egyptians so obstinate that they will go in after them." The Lord swept the sea with a strong east wind throughout the night and so turned it into dry land. When the water was thus divided, the Israelites marched into the midst of the sea on dry land, with the water like a wall to their right and to their left. The Egyptians followed in pursuit; all Pharaoh's horses and chariots and charioteers went after them right into the midst of the sea. And [the Lord] so clogged their chariot wheels that they could hardly drive. Then the Lord told Moses: "Stretch out your hand over the sea, that the water may flow back upon the Egyptians, upon their chariots and their charioteers." As the water flowed back, it covered Pharaoh's whole army which had followed the*

Israelites into the sea. Not a single one of them escaped. Thus the Lord saved Israel on that day from the power of the Egyptians. When Israel saw the Egyptians lying dead on the seashore and beheld the great power that the Lord had shown, they feared the Lord and believed in him and in his servant Moses. Then [they] sang this song to the Lord: I will sing to the Lord, for he is gloriously triumphant; horse and chariot he has cast into the sea.

Reflection:

On the night the Pharaoh finally "let my people go" they spoke of their mighty Lord, who with outstretched arm led them forth out of slavery and on their way to freedom. Now it's Moses, God's right-hand man, whose outstretched arm channels the power of God on their behalf. It was an awesome sight, to look back and see the once-powerful army that had chased after them, now a pile of corpses washing up on the shore. No wonder they feared God and pledged to follow Moses. (We'll see how long their enthusiasm lasts... about as long as ours, after we've begun our Lenten resolutions?) By the way, there is a story of a wise old rabbi who, in repeating this tale, pauses at the end to ask, "What is that sound we hear now?" When none of his listeners answers, he tells them, "That's the sound of the Lord, weeping over his dead Egyptian children...."

Fourth Reading

Isaiah 54: 5-14 *The Lord calls you back, like a wife forsaken and grieved in spirit. / For a brief moment I abandoned you, but with great tenderness I will take you back. / In an outburst of wrath, for a* *moment I hid my face from you; / but with enduring love I take pity on you, says the Lord, your redeemer. / My love shall never leave you nor my covenant of peace be shaken, says the Lord, who has mercy on you. / Great shall be the peace of your children. / In justice shall you be established, far from the fear of oppression.*

Reflection:
The people returning from Exile find their homeland in ruins. But God promises them a new beginning, a renewed covenant. Now that they've learned their lesson, he'll come close once more, and this time (if they're smart) he'll never (have to) leave them again!

Fifth Reading
Isaiah 55: 1-11 *Thus says the Lord: All you who are thirsty, come to the water! / Listen, that you may have life. / I will renew with you the everlasting covenant, the benefits assured to David. / Seek the Lord while he may be found, call him while he is near. / Turn to the Lord for mercy; to our God, who is generous in forgiving. / For my thoughts are not your thoughts, nor are your way my ways, says the Lord. / As high as the heavens are above the earth, so high are my ways above your ways and my thoughts above your thoughts. / For just as from the heavens the rain and snow come down / and do not return there till they have watered the earth, making it fertile and fruitful, / giving seed to him who sows and bread to him who eats, / so shall my word be that goes forth from my mouth; / it shall not return to me void, but shall do my will, achieving the end for which I sent it.*

Reflection:

Once again God reassures his people that, just because they mistakenly chose to wander away from his loving care and got into trouble, they don't have to be gun-shy: his offer still holds! So you broke the covenant—don't sweat it, I can renew it! I don't think like you do; I'm not full of resentment. I'm not going to say: "I tried to help you, but noooo, you wouldn't listen to me." You can come close and start over, and it will all come true again. Because when I say something, it gets done: maybe not right away, but it will happen, you have my word on it.

Sixth Reading

Baruch 3: 9-15, 32 – 4:4 *Hear, O Israel, the commandments of life: listen, and know prudence. / How is it, Israel, that you are in the land of your foes, grown old in a foreign land? / You have forsaken the fountain of wisdom! / Had you walked in the way of God, you would have dwelt in enduring peace. / Our God has traced out all the way of understanding, and has given her to Jacob, his servant, to Israel his beloved son. / She is the book of the precepts of God, the law that endures forever; / all who cling to her will live, but those will die who forsake her. / Turn, O Jacob, and receive her; walk by her light toward splendor. / Blessed are we, O Israel, for what pleases God is known to us!*

Reflection:

The prophet Baruch reminds his charges that the reason they were exiled was that they had abandoned the ways of God's law, the only wise way to live. You know the answers, they're in the Book.

So you live in misery? Put it all behind you. Start over, and cling to his precepts so that no harm will befall you.

Seventh Reading

Ezekiel 36: 16-28 *[The Lord says,] I scattered them among the nations, dispersing them over foreign lands; according to their conduct and deeds I judged them. But say to the house of Israel: for the sake of my holy name, I will gather you from all the foreign lands and bring you back to your own land. I will sprinkle clean water upon you to cleanse you from all your impurities, and from all your idols I will cleanse you. I will give you a new heart and place a new spirit within you, taking from your bodies your stony hearts and giving you natural hearts. I will put my spirit within you and make you live by my statutes, careful to observe my decrees. You shall live in the land I gave your fathers; you shall be my people, and I will be your God.*

Reflection:

Not that we deserve it, but from loyalty to his word to us, God will stay true to us, and come to our salvation. He'll play doctor and do a heart transplant, removing our dead, calcified hearts, and putting in a fresh new heart of flesh, so we can start living, and loving, again. We've stopped breathing, so he'll pinch our noses and put his mouth on ours and give us his breath ("my spirit") so our lungs and our new hearts can start pumping and beating again! Not only that: he'll give us back the home (in heaven) which we had lost, so we can start all over again. Just how clearly can he depict the New Covenant of Love that his Son will come to offer us?

[A historical aside: Early in the church's history, these Old Testament readings would be followed immediately by baptism, probably reflecting a time when they were the main ingredients in the preparation of new members. Remember, we were taking in converts way before what would be collected into the New Testament was all gathered together. Nowadays, we follow these O.T. readings with a sung <u>Gloria</u> (tonight with jubilant bells rung during its singing) and the opening prayer, then the readings of the Mass as usual.]

<u>Epistle</u>

Romans 6: 3-11 *Are you not aware that we who were baptized into Christ Jesus were baptized into his death? Through baptism into his death we were buried with him, so that, just as Christ was raised from the dead by the glory of the Father, we too might live a new life. If we have died with Christ, we believe that we are also to live with him. His death was death to sin, once for all; his life is life for God. In the same way, you must consider yourselves dead to sin but alive for God in Christ Jesus.*

Responsorial Psalm 118: 1-2, 16, 17, 22-23

Luke 24: 1-12 *On the first day of the week, at dawn, the women came to the tomb bringing the spices they had prepared. They found the stone rolled back; but when they entered the tomb, they did not find the body of the Lord Jesus. Two men in dazzling white garments appeared beside them [and] said to them: "Why do you search for the living One among the dead? He is not here; he has been raised.*

Remember what he said to you—that [he] must be delivered [and] crucified and on the third day rise again." With this reminder, his words came back to them.

Reflection:

Is baptism basic enough for you? It's not just starting over—it's really starting anew! We thought (so to speak) we were living when they brought us home from the maternity ward; it turns out that was just a poor imitation of living, that would come to an end when our bodies wore out. At our baptism we are born into Life with a capital L, a life that has no end, that calls us to heaven to be with God and all his loved ones, beyond all time! But we can't start to live that life until we die to the appearances of life here on earth. Just as we can't receive the Lord at communion until we recognize that it's more than just a piece of bread.

Isn't it funny how we can know something and still not know it? When the angels reminded the women of Jesus' foretelling his death and rising, they had an "aha!" experience and lost their fear and astonishment. They went right back to Peter and the assembly to give them the word. Here we know, thanks to our baptism, that we don't belong to this world, that we have in fact died to it, and still we so often let it impinge on our thinking and control our decisions. We live in Christ, not in the world. We belong to Christ, not to the world. We must put aside our fears, then, and act like Christ, not like the world.

III. The Rite of Initiation: Baptism, Confirmation, Eucharist

After the readings (and the homily) are over, the Litany of the Saints invokes the presence of our older brothers and sisters, our heroes in the faith, as we go to bless a new supply of water in preparation for baptisms. The water will produce life by the action of the Holy Spirit, so we beg for the Father to send his breath of life, his Spirit—just as in Genesis life springs from the spirit of God fructifying the waters. The baptismal font is compared to a womb, the womb of the holy church which will bear God holy children, first born into this life, but now born into God's own life as his new creation. In blessing the baptismal water, the presider plunges the paschal candle into the water (three times, of course) in a none-too-subtle phallic bit to show that the waters of the font derive their power to pass on the Spirit's power and life from the passion/death/resurrection of Christ. A little of the holy chrism is also poured into the water to signify its hallowing by the Holy Spirit.

In his revision of this rite Pius XII insisted that this blessing take place inside the sanctuary, so that everyone could see it and hear it. He also recommended that at this time at least one candidate be baptized, so we could all witness the working out of the ritual. Today many parishes enjoy the culmination of the RCIA (Rite of Christian Initiation of Adults) by witnessing the baptism of the catechumens from their own ranks, new brothers and sisters who will join their parish in the following of Christ. Naturally, this initiation is continued through their Confirmation and first Eucharist as the Mass continues.

But whether this takes place or not, the restored Vigil of Easter calls for all the faithful to join in the renewal of baptismal promises (ideally, accompanying our newly baptized). The readings, the water, and the witnessing of baptisms, all bring us to recall and renew the promises that were originally made for most of us by our godparents. Now's our chance, at the most fitting time and place, to re-commit our lives in a conscious and heart-felt response to the great goodness of God in making us his own.

The church asks us to renew our rejection of sin and our accept-ance of the new life Christ offers us. Like the "I do" of a couple that's celebrating their 25th anniversary, our "I do" must look to the past, with lessons learned from all its ups and downs, and to the future, with a renewed confidence based on the ever-growing awareness of the meaning of that ceremony long ago. The whole Lenten observance was intended to prepare us for a genuine, sincere re-commitment to our following of Christ. Think of the deepening of patriotic feelings when you watch a friend become a citizen and now swear allegiance to the country that has meant so much to you. This is the point of the renewal of our baptismal promises, and, to make it more real to us, the celebrant sprinkles us with the Easter water that brought us to life.

IV. Liturgy of the Eucharist

The Eucharist is the paschal mystery in an easy-to-take, capsule form. It has been said that no other way of celebrating our redemption, however beautiful or meaningful, can take its place. Every Sunday is called a "little Easter." In fact, everything that takes place in this Easter Vigil is only an unfolding of what is celebrated every day in the mystery of the Eucharist, at plain ol' daily Mass. Singing the triple Alleluia after the epistle in the Masses of the Easter season, plus adding a double Alleluia to the chanted dismissal, gives us a neat and welcome chance to prolong our joyful praise of God.

Five

SUNDAY OF THE LORD'S RESURRECTION
Introduction

This Mass is a post script if there ever was one. It came about as a means of covering those Catholics who could not make it with the rest of the community to the Mass of Easter par excellence, the Vigil celebration. In the earliest days of the church, nobody needed it: for the Jews (and that's what almost all of Jesus' first followers were) Sunday begins as of sunset of Saturday. That's how they counted the three days of Jesus in his tomb: starting Friday before sundown (that's one), all day Saturday (that's two), and then half of Sunday—by morning light he was gone, but he had been in since Saturday's sunset (that's three—you're out!). For them, their full participation, and full attendance, at the Vigil of Easter on Holy Saturday night was the observance of Easter.

As time passed, we grew in numbers and changed in thinking, pushing the celebrations forward in time. Certainly by the Middle Ages, when Saturday's service began in the morning, there was no doubt the Sunday service was absolutely necessary. With the reform of the rite came the re-placement of the Vigil service at night, in the dark. So the feast recovered its special glamour and function, but it would not replace the Sunday observance of the feast of Easter, which, never intended as unique, naturally was repeated as many times as necessary through the whole day.

By the way, from the start there was a dispute about when Easter fell. You see, the Jewish Passover fell always on the 14th day of the month of Nisan, regardless of what day of the week it was. For our early converts from Judaism, this was a natural. Christians who were more excited about the celebration of Jesus' resurrection than the memorial of his death, would naturally prefer a Sunday, celebrating the day of his rising to new life! By 325, the Council of Nicea stipulated that it would be the first Sunday after the first full moon after the spring equinox. This means it is a moveable feast: it can occur anywhere from the 22nd of March to the 25th of April. (Eastern Christians prefer the old Julian calendar to its Gregorian reform, and their Easter usually falls after ours by a few weeks.)

Scripture and Reflection

Acts of the Apostles 10: 34, 37-43 *Peter [said], "You know what has been reported all over Judea about Jesus, of the way God anointed* *him with the Holy Spirit and power. He went about doing good and healing. And God was with him. We are witnesses to all he did. They killed him finally, 'hanging him on a tree,' only to have God raise him up on the third day and grant that he be seen by witnesses chosen by God—by us who ate and drank with him after he rose. To him all the prophets testify, that everyone who believes in him has forgiveness of sins through his name."*

Responsorial Psalm 118: 1-2, 16-17, 22-23

Colossians 3: 1-4 *Since you have been raised up with Christ, set your heart on what pertains to higher realms where Christ is seated at God's right hand. Be intent on things above rather than on things of earth. After all, you have died! Your life is hidden now with Christ in God. When Christ our life appears, then you shall appear with him in glory.*

(OR alternate epistle – 1 Corinthians 5: 6-8 *Do you not know that a little yeast has its effect all through the dough? Get rid of the old yeast to make of yourselves fresh dough, unleavened loaves, as it were. Christ our Passover has been sacrificed. Let us celebrate the feast not with the old yeast, that of corruption and wickedness, but with the unleavened bread of sincerity and truth.)*

John 20: 1-9 *Early in the morning on the first day of the week, while it was still dark, Mary Magdalene came to the tomb. She saw that the stone had been moved away, so she ran off to Simon Peter and the other disciple (the one Jesus loved) and told them, "The Lord has been taken from the tomb! We don't know where they have put him!" At that,*

Peter and the other disciple started out toward the tomb. They were running, but the other disciple reached the tomb first. He did not enter but bent down to peer in, and saw the wrappings lying on the ground. Peter came and entered the tomb. He observed the wrappings on the ground and saw the piece of cloth which had covered the head not lying with the wrappings, but rolled up by itself. Then the [other] disciple went in. He saw and believed. (Remember, as yet they did not understand the Scripture that Jesus had to rise from the dead.)

Reflection:

This selection from Acts is one of the earliest capsule-form proclamations (kerygma in Greek) of the Good News about Jesus. Listeners whose interest was piqued and wanted to learn more about it would then come and receive further teaching (didache) or instruction (catechesis) and, when committed, would become catechumens (wannabes, in training) and eventually members of the church at their baptism.

Paul reminds the Colossians that, having died and risen with Christ, they must no longer be concerned with the things of earth, but live intent on things above, where they belong, "with Christ in God."

(Alternate epistle, 1 Corinthians: Yeast (leaven) was forbidden in the Passover week (Exodus 12: 18-20) to remember the haste in which they ate the sacrificed lamb that night while awaiting the signal to flee their homes in Egypt—there was no time for the bread to rise, so they ate it unleavened. Every Jewish home had to get rid of all its yeast, and then a week later start over with a fresh supply. In their culture, there was generally a negative connotation to yeast; they considered its effect on bread to come from its own decomposition/corruption.)

John's gospel presents two episodes at the empty tomb of Jesus. Mary Magdalene makes the initial discovery and goes for Peter and the other disciple. They race out to the tomb (the younger outraces the older, but defers to his seniority) to see for themselves. One sees, the other sees and believes.

[With the Renewal of Baptismal Promises following the service of the word, the community's shared profession of faith becomes obviously redundant, and is dropped.]

Six
FEASTS FOLLOWING EASTER

THE ASCENSION OF THE LORD

Scripture and Reflections

(A-B-C) Acts of the Apostles 1: 1-11 *My first account dealt with all that Jesus did and taught until the day he was taken up to heaven, having first instructed the apostles through the Holy Spirit. In the time after his suffering he showed them in many convincing ways that he was alive, appearing to them over the course of forty days. On one occasion he told them not to leave Jerusalem: "Wait, rather, for the fulfillment of my Father's promise. John baptized with water, but within a few days you will be baptized with the Holy Spirit. You will receive power when the Holy Spirit comes down on you, then you are to be my witnesses in Jerusalem, even to the ends of the earth."*

No sooner had he said this than he was lifted up before their eyes in a cloud which took him from their sight.

Responsorial Psalm   47: 2-3, 6-7, 8-9

(A-B-C) Ephesians 1: 17-23 *May the God of our Lord Jesus Christ grant you a spirit of wisdom and insight to know him clearly...and the immeasurable scope of his power in us who believe. It is like the strength he showed in raising Christ from the dead and seating him at his right hand in heaven, high above every principality, power, virtue and domination, and every name that can be given in this age or the age to come. He has put all things under Christ's feet and has made him thus exalted, head of the church, which is his body, the fullness of him who fills the universe in all its parts.*

Cycle A
Matthew 28: 16-20 *The eleven made their way to Galilee [and] Jesus addressed them: "Go and make disciples of all nations. Baptize them in the name 'of the Father, and of the Son, and of the Holy Spirit.' Teach them to carry out everything I have commanded you. And know that I am with you always, until the end of the world."*

Reflection:
The end of the first Gospel commissions them to baptize and teach with the authority of Jesus himself, who will be with them, and with the church, till the end of time. The quotations around the Trinitarian formula in the text are explained in a footnote in the

Jerusalem Bible: It may be that this formula, so far as the fullness of its expression is concerned, is a reflection of the liturgical usage established later in the primitive community, meaning that the words we've grown accustomed to using are placed on the lips of Jesus when this comes to be written down.

Cycle B

Mark 16: 15-20 *[Jesus appeared to the Eleven and] said to them: "Go into the whole world and proclaim the good news to all creation." Then the Lord Jesus was taken up into heaven and took his seat at God's right hand. The Eleven went forth and preached everywhere. The Lord continued to work with them throughout and confirm the message through the signs which accompanied them.*

Reflection:

This is the conclusion to the second Gospel. Notice how Mark interweaves the great events of Jesus' resurrection, ascension, exaltation, taking his place at the Father's right hand, and receiving the title "Lord." This title encompasses and caps off all of Jesus' career, which is now visibly present and at work through his disciples, in his church.

Cycle C

Luke 24: 46-53 *Jesus said to the Eleven: "See, I send down upon you the promise of my Father. Remain here in the city until you are clothed with power from on high." He then led them out near Bethany, and blessed them. As he blessed, he left them, and was taken up to heaven.*

Reflection:

Luke's Jesus insists, both at the end of volume I (Gospel) and at the start of volume II (Acts), that the apostles wait in Jerusalem for the empowering by the Holy Spirit that the Father will send them. Jesus is closing the cover on his own book, but wants them ready for the next volume—the coming of the Spirit upon them. Looking back, it's pretty darned obvious, but that's hindsight for you. They will be quite surprised by the Spirit's arrival, in the loud wind blowing and the tongues as of fire settling over them. The real surprise, of course, will be for the world. "Who are those guys?" (a la Sundance Kid) – there's no stopping them! Our timorous, cowering disciples are coming bravely into the open and preaching their heads off, once the Spirit's power has been unleashed in them.

Paul sings a hymn of lyric praise to Jesus, the head of the body of believers, raised from the dead, and now raised from earth to heaven, so he can be seen in his rightful place—at the right hand of God, over every creature, filling the entire universe with the glory that the Father has given him.

[A historical aside:

The entire 50-day period following Easter was originally called Pentecost (in Greek, fiftieth {day is understood}, in Latin Quinquagesima) but over time the first 40 days were considered a sort of after-Lent, the time of the risen Christ with his disciples until his Ascension. The last 10 days form a prelude for the descent of the Holy Spirit. Prior to this partitioning, Easter was considered to contain the entire paschal mystery: death, resurrection, ascension, and the sending of the Spirit.]

THE VIGIL OF PENTECOST

Scripture and Reflections

(A-B-C)
(four choices for the first reading:)
1st – Genesis 11: 1-9 *At that time the whole world spoke the same language. [The people] said, "Let us build ourselves a city and a tower with its top in the sky, and so make a name for ourselves; otherwise we shall be scattered all over the earth." The Lord came down to see [it and] said, "If now, while they are one people, speaking the same language, they have started to do this, nothing will later stop them from doing whatever they presume to do. Let us then go down and confuse their language, so that no one will understand what another says." That is why it was called Babel, because there the Lord confused the speech of all the world [and] scattered them all over the earth.*

2nd – Exodus 19: 3-8, 16-20 *Moses went up the mountain to God. The Lord said, "Tell the Israelites: 'You have seen for yourselves how I treated the Egyptians and how I bore you up on eagle wings and brought you here to myself. If you hearken to my voice and keep my covenant, you shall be my special possession, dearer to me than all other people.'" So Moses went and summoned the people. When he [told] them all that the Lord had ordered, the people all answered* together, *"Everything the Lord has said, we will do."* On the third day Moses led the people out of the camp to meet God, and they stationed themselves at the foot of Mount Sinai [which] was all wrapped in smoke, for the Lord came down upon it in fire, and the whole mountain trembled violently.

3rd – Ezekiel 37: 1-14 *The hand of the Lord led me out in the spirit of the Lord and set me in the center of the plain, which was filled with bones. He said to me: Prophesy over these bones, and say to them: Dry bones, hear the word of the Lord! Thus says the Lord God to these bones: I will bring spirit into you, that you may come to life. I will put sinews upon you, make flesh grow over you, cover you with skin, and put spirit in you so that you may come to life and know that I am the Lord. As I was prophesying I heard a noise; it was a rattling as the bones came together. I saw the sinews and the flesh come upon them, and the skin cover them, but there was no spirit in them. Then he said to me: Prophesy and say to the spirit: Thus says the Lord God: Come, O spirit, and breathe into these slain that they may come to life. And the spirit came into them; they came alive and stood upright, a vast army. Then he said to me: These bones are the whole house of Israel. They have been saying, "Our bones are dried up, our hope is lost, and we are cut off." Say to them: Thus says the Lord: O my people, I will open your graves and have you rise from them, and bring you back to the land of Israel. Then you shall know that I am the Lord. I will put my spirit in you that you may live, and I will settle you upon your land, thus you shall know that I am the Lord. I have promised, and I will do it, says the Lord.*

4th – Joel 3: 1-5 *Thus says the Lord: I will pour out my spirit upon all mankind. / Your sons and daughters shall prophesy, your old men shall dream dreams, your young men shall see visions; / even upon the servants and handmaids I will pour out my spirit. / The sun will be turned to darkness, and the moon to blood, / at the coming of the Day of the Lord, the great and terrible day. / Then everyone shall be rescued who calls on the name of the Lord; / for on Mount Zion there shall be a remnant, as the Lord has said, / and in Jerusalem survivors whom the Lord shall call.*

Responsorial Psalm 104: 1-2, 24, 27-28, 29, 30

Romans 8:22-27 *The Spirit helps us in our weakness, for we do not know how to pray as we ought; but the Spirit himself makes intercession for us with groanings which cannot be expressed in speech. He who searches hearts knows what the Spirit means, for the Spirit intercedes for the saints as God himself wills.*

John 7:37-39 *Jesus [said], "If anyone thirsts, let him come to me; let him drink. Scripture has it: 'From within him rivers of living water shall flow.'" (He was referring to the Spirit, whom those that came to believe in him were to receive. There was no Spirit as yet, since Jesus had not yet been glorified.)*

Reflection:

1st – At Pentecost, the Holy Spirit will become the unifier of all people, by undoing the Babel experience. The language of God's love will overcome all barriers and gather all people from the world over into the one flock under one Shepherd.

2nd – At Pentecost, without the smoke and trembling, the Holy Spirit will establish a new covenant with the new people of God, Jesus' little band of followers all gathered in the upper room. The tongues of fire clearly supply the sign of God's approving partnership.

3rd – At Pentecost, God's breath of life, his spirit, will blow over the lifeless panorama of this sinful world, and bring a new life—God's own—into what without him would be just a bunch of old bleached bones lying around. We can come back from our sins: "I have promised, and I will do it, says the Lord."

4th – The Lord promises: "I will pour out my spirit upon all mankind. Your sons and daughters shall prophesy, your old men shall dream dreams, your young men shall see visions." And in case you thought he was being stingy with his spirit, "Even upon the servants and the handmaids, I will pour out my spirit." Does that about cover it? God wants to share his life-giving breath (the Spirit) with everyone.

St. Paul reassures us, that even if we can't do as good a job of praying as we should, the Holy Spirit within us takes over and goes above and beyond what the finest of human words could accomplish. He's on the same frequency as the Father, who reads him like a lovely book.

At the festival of Tabernacles (Booths) there is a blessing of God for his gift of water, the most precious commodity for desert dwellers. From this background comes Jesus' allusion to rivers of living water, likely hearkening back to Ezekiel's vision of the water that begins as a trickle from the Temple door and then becomes a mighty, life-giving river (chapter 47). We also remember Jesus in conversation with the Samaritan woman at the well in John's chapter 4, assuring her of never-ending supplies of living water. At Calvary John (19: 35) will make much of the water he witnessed coming out of Jesus' pierced heart. St. Paul will establish a powerful image, connecting the life-giving waters of baptism with the "pouring out" of the Holy Spirit upon us.

PENTECOST: MASS DURING THE DAY

Scripture and Reflections

(A-B-C)

Acts of the Apostles 2: 1-11 *[On] the day of Pentecost the brethren [were] gathered in one place. Suddenly from up in the sky there came a noise like a strong, driving wind which was heard throughout the house. Tongues as of fire appeared which parted and came to rest on each of them. All were filled with the Holy Spirit. They began to express themselves in foreign tongues and make bold proclamations as the Spirit prompted them. Staying in Jerusalem at the time were devout Jews of every nation under heaven. These heard the sound, and* *assembled in a large crowd. They were much confused because each of them heard these men speaking his own language. The whole occurrence astonished them.*

Responsorial Psalm 104: 1, 24, 29-30, 31, 34

1 Corinthians 12: 3-7, 12-13 *No one can say, "Jesus is Lord," except by the Holy Spirit. There are different kinds of spiritual gifts but the same Spirit; there are different workings but the same God who produces all of them in everyone. For in one Spirit we were all baptized into one body, whether Jews or Greeks, slaves or free persons, and we were all given to drink of one Spirit.*

(alternate second reading) Romans 8: 8-17 *If Christ is in you, although the body is dead because of sin, the spirit is alive because of righteousness. If the Spirit of the one who raised Jesus from the dead dwells in you, the one who raised Christ from the dead will give life to your mortal bodies also, through his Spirit that dwells in you. Those who are led by the Spirit of God are sons of God. For you did not receive a spirit of slavery to fall back into fear, but you received a spirit of adoption, through whom we cry, "Abba, Father!"*

John 20: 19-23 *On the evening of that first day of the week, Jesus came and said to them, "Peace be with you. As the Father has sent me, so I send you." [Then] he breathed on them and said, "Receive the Holy Spirit."*

(alternate Gospel reading) John 14: 15-16, 23-26 *Jesus said to his disciples: "I will ask the Father, and he will give you another Advocate to be with you always. Whoever loves me will keep my word, and my Father will love him, and we will come to him and make our dwelling with him. I have told you this while I am with you. The Advocate, the Holy Spirit whom the Father will send in my name, will teach you everything and remind you of all that I told you."*

Background:
The term "economy of salvation" was coined centuries ago by theologians to describe the activity of God in the working out of our salvation. They speak of the three eras, or stages, in accord with the activity of each of the three Persons of God. The first is the age of the Father, whose main role is creation. Then, at the appointed time, Jesus appears in our history as our redeemer. Whereas the era of the Creator covered eons, the era of the Redeemer comprised just around thirty-some years. Not a lot of time, but a very concentrated dose of salvation! Finally, we come to the age of the Spirit, whose role is to be our Sanctifier. Only God knows how long this period will go on, but we know when it started: when Jesus left us to go to the Father and send us another Paraclete (Advocate), who would take over the work in its plan C. Interesting, no?

Obviously, all three Persons in the Trinity share intimately in all of God's work, but, for purposes of discussion and analysis, we have to use our limited (and therefore limiting) human thought patterns. Thus we "separate" the activities of the three divine Persons into neat packets that allow us to "capture" a little bit of clarification. We could, of course, just throw up our hands and say it's all a mystery, but I think it's good for us to use the brains God gave us and try to advance in our understanding of the Trinitarian mystery—the most basic truth about God revealed to us. We now return to our regularly scheduled program.

Reflection:

In his gospel and the Book of Acts, St. Luke has produced a two-volume set on the activity of the Holy Spirit. The first deals with the Spirit at work in Jesus: present at his conception, at his presentation at the temple, at the baptism which opens his career, all through his life, and returned to the Father's hands at the moment of Jesus' death. The second volume charters the same activities of the same Spirit in the not-quite-the-same Jesus: the Jesus who lives in his body, the church. Today's Acts 2 marks the birthday of the church as we exist today: Jesus seemingly absent but powerfully and sacramentally present in the actions of his body, the assembly of his followers who constitute his real, bodily, corporate presence by the action of his Spirit at work in us.

In Acts 2 we see the antidote for Genesis 11's scattering of humanity into different language groups ("he has scattered the proud in their conceit"). Now begins the great project of the re-unifying of the whole world ("to the ends of the earth" we are to witness), based on the Spirit's power at work in us. Isn't the job of the Holy Spirit to be the glue of love between Father and

Son? Doesn't the Spirit provide the same wonderful effect for us when we become brothers and sisters of Jesus?

St. Paul's first selection reminds us that the same God is the source of our life, and of all our gifts. We are given these gifts, not for an exclusive use/enjoyment, but for the good of all the members of the one body we form by being "all baptized into one body." Caught up in the language of baptismal imagery, he liquefies the ethereal breath of God into the living water "we were all given to drink."

In Romans 8 we are swept up into the Trinitarian life of God. Since Christ is in us, the Spirit in which he was raised up from death by the Father will also raise us up. Thus, the Spirit we've received is a spirit of adoption, making us sons and daughters of God just as truly as Jesus is God's Son! This opens our approach of filial love for God, so we "dare to say" (as the intro to the Lord's Prayer encourages): not "Your Excellency," or "Sovereign Lord," or "Omnipotent, All-knowing Majesty, Who maintainest all things in their proper order..." but simply and lovingly "Abba, Father!" Ah, the Spirit, bond of love!

John 19 makes the meaning of the word "spirit" transparent: Jesus breathes on us and says, "Receive the Holy Spirit (the Holy Breath of Life...and not just human life, but the life that the Father and I share)." Mi casa es su casa.

In John 14, Jesus is preparing his disciples (unsuccessfully, as usual) for his "leaving" them behind. Poor babies, they were crushed when his death took him from them, elated when he returned, and loath to see him go away again. But how consoling is the promise of Jesus "my Father will love him, and we will come to him <u>and make our dwelling with him</u>" (emphasis added). Remember that lovely phrase of yesteryear—the Indwelling of the Holy Spirit? That's what the Spirit does for us as our Sanctifier: he introduces us into the Trinitarian life of God, here and now, right in the middle of this messy world! This is why we can say (and mean): Jesus Christ is Lord! The Creator is my Abba! Thank you, Holy Spirit.

And now it is my bittersweet duty to remind us (I feel like the guy who put the last stone on the Taj Mahal—hey, great! but now it's all over....) that we've come to the end of the great Paschal season, the Church's great retreat, that got us on board all the way from Ash Wednesday along the sorrowful but purposeful journey with Jesus, through the intense events of Palm Sunday and the Triduum, and—onward and upward!—along the way of Jesus raised from death and rising to heaven, to send us the Spirit, the mission of his entire life's work. Pentecost is not an isolated feast. It was the motive for Jesus' work as Redeemer, so he could pass on the baton as we pass over into our new Christian life in the Spirit, the Sanctifier. The Pentecostal arrival of the Holy Spirit, who picks up where Christ left off, marks the beginning of the final stage of our life, the birth of the church. Happy Birthday, everybody! Alleluia! Amen.

MOST HOLY TRINITY SUNDAY

Introduction

This is only <u>the</u> foundational truth about God, so what am I doing strapping on diving gear and going into the deep? Well, it was Frank Sheed who impressed me long ago with this image of "mystery": we can see it as a locked door, impervious to attack, unyielding of any of the secrets within, totally beyond our ability to comprehend/take in...or, we can picture it as an art gallery full of breathtakingly beautiful objects, so many that we'll <u>never</u>—literally—<u>never</u> (we lack the time/possibility) make it all the way to the end of this loooooong hallway full of exhibits. Either way, it's beyond our comprehension, it's a mystery. But if we attempt to go as far as we can, we'll be discovering, perhaps not beauty in its entirety, but certainly a lot of beautiful bits! And so, let's see what insights we can glean from this tremendous mystery of God's Triune Being.

As far as we know, every culture has always acknowledged a force superior to itself, usually pictured as being above us, in the heavens (though at times in the nether regions as well). People, in their helplessness, have always felt the need to ask for help from the superior being(s) looking down on their bumbling, problem-filled lives. We try to get them to listen to us with offerings, prayers, rituals, etc. To make a long story short, the Jews received the revelation of Yahweh's existence and (marvelously!)

benevolent interest in them. Jesus will know this faraway God as his Father.

We come to find out that Jesus is really Emmanuel, God-with-us, within reach! What an advance: from God off in the distance to a God who walks and talks and eats with us! But wait, it gets better: Jesus wants us to experience the intimacy he feels with the Father, so he finds a way to make God even closer—from God above (Father) to God beside (Jesus) to God within! (the Spirit). Jesus "abandons" us as he takes leave in the ascension, but he does not leave us orphans. From his rightful place at the throne of God, he and the Father send us the powerful inward presence of our Advocate. Talk about an approachable God! He speaks to us, listens to us, prays with and for us, accompanies our every step, sparks our every heartbeat...(stop me!). What a love-ly evolution in our awareness of God and our mutual relationship.

Scripture and Reflections

Scripture: Cycle A

Exodus 34: 4-6, 8-9 *Having come down in a cloud, the Lord passed before [Moses at Mount Sinai] and cried out, "The Lord, a merciful and gracious God, slow to anger and rich in kindness and fidelity." Moses at once bowed down in worship [and] said, "If I find favor with you, O Lord, do come along in our company. This is indeed a stiff-necked people; yet pardon our wickedness and sins, and receive us as your own."*

Responsorial Psalm: Daniel 3: 52-56

2 Corinthians 13: 11-13 *Live in harmony and peace, and the God of love and peace will be with you. The grace of the Lord Jesus Christ, and the love of God, and the fellowship of the Holy Spirit be with you all!*

John 3: 16-18 *God so loved the world that he gave his only son, that whoever believes in him may not die but may have eternal life.*

Reflection:

From the start, we learn to put our faith in what God reveals about himself: his mercy, kindness and fidelity. God will continue to reveal more of himself to us along our journey, through the prophets, and finally in and through his Son, who reveals that faith in him brings us to the eternal life God has offered us in our covenant partnership. Paul's greeting calls us to live in harmony (3-part? Trinitarian?), love and peace. His explicit reference to the three persons of God is one of the choices of greetings for our use at Mass.

Scripture: Cycle B

Deuteronomy 4: 32-34, 39-40 *Moses said to the people: "Did any god take a nation for himself, by signs and wonders, with his strong hand and outstretched arm, all of which the Lord, your God, did for you in Egypt before your very eyes? This is why you must know, and fix in your heart, that the Lord is God in the heavens above and on earth* *below, and that there is no other. You must keep his commandments, that you may have long life on the land which the Lord, your God, is giving you forever."*

Responsorial Psalm 33:   4-5, 6, 9, 18-19, 20, 22

Romans 8:14-17 *All who are led by the Spirit of God are sons of God. You did not receive a spirit of slavery leading you back into fear, but a spirit of adoption through which we cry out, "Abba!" (that is, "Father"). We are children of God, heirs with Christ.*

Matthew 28: 16-20   [This selection has appeared (and been reflected on) in the Cycle A readings for the Feast of the Ascension of the Lord. Please see page 70.]

Cycle C
Proverbs 8: 22-31 *Thus says the wisdom of God: "The Lord possessed me, / from of old I was poured forth, at the first, before the earth. / When [the Lord] made firm the skies above, when he set for the sea its limit, / then was I beside him as his craftsman, and I was his delight day by day, / playing before him all the while, playing on the surface of his earth; / and I found delight in the human race."*

Responsorial Psalm 8: 4-5, 6-7, 8-9

Romans 5: 1-5 *Now that we have been justified by faith, we are at peace with God through our Lord Jesus Christ. Through him, we have* *gained access by faith to the grace in which we now stand, and we boast of our hope for the glory of God...because the love of God has been poured out in our hearts through the Holy Spirit who has been given to us.*

John 16: 12-15 *Jesus said to his disciples: "I have much more to tell you, but you cannot bear it now. When he comes, however, being the Spirit of truth he will guide you to all truth...because he will have received from me what he will announce to you. All that the Father has belongs to me. That is why I said that what he will announce to you he will have from me."*

Reflection:

In Proverbs, the virtue of wisdom is personified. In fact, the word "wisdom" in Greek is Sophia—personal enough for you? She is depicted as accompanying the Creator God on his rounds as he gets things going, and she's having fun playing around with all the new toys! Christians happily applied this personification to the Holy Spirit. And, of course, Jesus is present as well, as the pattern for all of creation, the model for all the rest of the Father's children.

The selection from Romans mentions explicitly the three Persons of the Trinity. We are at peace with God the Father through our Lord Jesus, who gives us access to the grace in which we now stand, and to the love of God that has been poured out in our hearts through the Holy Spirit. (Notice Paul's pronounced proclivity for baptismal/water imaging of the Spirit.)

In his Farewell Discourse at the Last Supper with his friends, Jesus mentions his relationships with the Spirit and the Father. The Spirit is in charge of guiding us to all truth, and that's what the Father has entrusted to his Son for our salvation. So Jesus delegates the Spirit to carry out his orders on our behalf. The intended intimacy with the Father which Jesus wants to share with us will be achieved in our active reception of, and co-operation with, the presence of the Spirit, who will accomplish for us (Jesus' brothers and sisters) what he accomplishes for the Son—union with the Father. This lovely circling and re-circling, ever more closely, is what theologians have called perichoresis, which translates as "dancing around" (chorus line, anyone?). Isn't it a neat picture of God—the three Persons dancing around each other? And guess who's invited to cut in?

CORPUS CHRISTI:
THE FEAST OF THE BODY AND BLOOD OF CHRIST

[BUT FIRST, A WORD ABOUT A WORD:
Yeah, "transubstantiation," you get points if you guessed it. In the old Roman Rite, most of the attention was directed to the objects of bread and wine, and to the reality of the Sacred Presence they contained, in response to the doctrinal attacks and heresies of the times. The challenge to the reality of Jesus' divine presence produced a huge, almost overstated insistence on how truly the all-holy, fully divine Jesus was there, in that little consecrated

wafer. That, in turn, produced a devotional distancing of the man-in-the-pew, since the times were also pretty harsh on our sinfulness. You would think sinners would be hungry to receive the strength of this holy food, but in fact they became so convinced of their unworthiness that they just stayed away. Often, only the priest celebrating the Mass would receive Communion.

Anyway, thanks to more level-headed thinking, and Pius X's agenda on encouraging the popular reception of Holy Communion, followed by Pius XII's relaxation of the Eucharistic fast, so more people could more readily receive, Catholics began to approach the rail in much greater numbers. The church, since it was no longer on the defensive, began calling our attention more to the <u>meaning</u> of the Eucharist. The weapon of choice for "explaining" this mystery was the teaching of St. Thomas Aquinas, who in turn based his thinking on Aristotle's thought patterns. An impressive line of credentials, eh? You begin by accepting the <u>terms</u> for discussion. For Aristotle, and now Thomas Aquinas, "substance" is the inner, non-visible essence of an object, what makes it be what it is. In juxtaposition, "accident" is any of the series of surface characteristics exhibited by any possessor of that "substance." (I know, I know, not fun, this philosophy business, but stick with it—it's good for the mind.)

An example should help right about now. Take "car" (but not when that little red light's flashing, or you'll set off the alarm). So many different vehicles come under this label: Mini-Coopers and Europe's SwatchCars to sub-compacts and compacts; through sedans and those land-yachts that had three-foot-long fins over the rear tires, all the way to Lincoln Navigators and Hummers and even stretch-limo Hummers (I once saw a white one waiting for the bridal party to come out from St. Mary's Basilica in downtown Phoenix). You get it? They sure have different meet-the-eye surface traits/"accidents" (hey, interesting choice for an example!), but essentially, they are all cars: they share the underlying "substance" of "car-ness."

You may breathe now. At Mass, when the priest says the words of Jesus, Christ's power will leave intact and observable all the outside, surface "accidents" of the host (its taste, shape, color, appearance—all the stuff we notice about it) while surgically removing its underlying, non-visible essence, its bread-ness, and replacing it with the "substance" of Jesus, our brother, the second Person of the Blessed Trinity. TRANS-substantiation describes the transfer out of one substance being replaced by another one transferring in, unnoticed because it takes place under the cover of the accidents that remain, that once belonged to the substance that has been replaced, namely, bread. So it looks like bread, it might even taste like bread, but it's Jesus! Yeah, well, you've got to have faith!

(There, aren't you glad we took that detour? You're not? Oops. Hey, I meant well. Aquinas, and the church for centuries afterward, thought it was the cat's pajamas.)

Scripture and Reflections

Cycle A

Deuteronomy 8: 2-3, 14-16 *Moses said to the people: "Remember the Lord your God fed you with manna, a food unknown to you and your fathers, to show you that not by bread alone does man live, but by every word that comes forth from the mouth of the Lord. He brought forth water for you from the flinty rock and fed you in the desert with manna."*

Responsorial Psalm 147: 12-13, 14-15, 19-20

1 Corinthians 10: 16-17 *Is not the cup of blessing we bless a sharing in the blood of Christ? And is not the bread we break a sharing in the body of Christ? Because the loaf of bread is one, we, many though we are, are one body for we all partake of the one loaf.*

John 6: 51-58 *Jesus said to the crowds of the Jews: "He who feeds on my flesh and drinks my blood has life eternal, and I will raise him up on the last day. [He] remains in me and I in him. Just as the Father who has life sent me and I have life because of the Father, so the man who feeds on me will have life because of me. This is the bread that came down from heaven. Unlike your ancestors who ate and died nonetheless, the man who feeds on this bread shall live forever."*

Reflection:

God is like a nursing mother to his people in the desert. Every day they must have recourse to his miraculously provided nourishment, enough to keep them strong for another day's journey.

This is obviously the "daily bread" to which Jesus alluded in his prayer given to the disciples. For Paul, our sharing in the body and blood of Christ at the Eucharist clearly makes us one. Many though we may seem to be, we come together like slices from one loaf, like sips from one cup. At every Mass, as we seem to be receiving "chunks" from the one loaf—just the reverse is happening—it is we who are in fact being "chunked together" into the one loaf of the body of Christ.

As so often in John's gospel, Jesus makes a bold proclamation which is promptly misunderstood by his listener(s). The ensuing objection allows Jesus to elucidate at length and tell more of what he really means. The miracle of the feeding in the desert did not go far enough: it met only the day's need, and only until they arrived at lands they could cultivate to produce their own food. The miracle of Jesus providing for our life is that he takes us beyond our life on earth to our life in heaven, our sharing in God's own life.

Scripture and Reflections

Cycle B

Exodus 24: 3-8 *Moses came to the people and related all the words and ordinances of the Lord, then he erected an altar and twelve pillars for the twelve tribes of Israel. He took half of the blood [of the sacrificed young bulls] and put it in large bowls; the other half he splashed on the altar. Taking the book of the covenant, he read it aloud to the people, who answered, "All that the Lord has said, we will* *heed and do." Then to took the blood and sprinkled it on the people, saying, "This is the blood of the covenant which the Lord has made with you."*

Responsorial Psalm 116: 12-13, 15-16, 17-18

Hebrews 9: 11-15 *When Christ came as high priest he entered not with the blood of goats and calves but with his own blood, and achieved eternal redemption. For if the blood of goats and bulls can sanctify those who are defiled so that their flesh is cleansed, how much more will the blood of Christ cleanse [us] from dead works to worship the living God! This is why he is mediator of a new covenant: since his death has taken place for deliverance from transgressions committed under the first covenant, those who are called may receive the promised eternal inheritance.*

Mark 14: 12-16, 22-26 *The disciples said to Jesus, "Where do you wish us to go to prepare the Passover supper for you?" He sent two [of them, saying], "Go into the city and you will come upon a man carrying a water jar. Follow him. Whatever house he enters, say to the owner, 'The Teacher asks, Where is my guest room where I may eat the Passover with my disciples?' He will show you a room, all in order." During the meal [Jesus] took bread, blessed and broke it, and gave it to them. "Take this," he said, "this is my body." He likewise took a cup, gave thanks and passed it to them, and they all drank from it. He said to them: "This is my blood, the blood of the covenant, to be poured out on behalf of many."*

Reflection:

In ancient times, a covenant was a recognized agreement, formalized by the sacrifice of animals, with their blood sprinkled on the participants to hold them both accountable. Here, since God is one of the partners, his half of the blood is poured out on the altar, and the other half is sprinkled on the people, ratifying their part of the covenant obligation. In <u>Hebrews</u>, Christ is the mediator of a new covenant, representing both parties: coming with love from God to us, and leading us back repentant to the Father. His blood is not just an indicator of the cleansing process—it actually brings it about! His bloody death brings us to Life.

Mark's gospel depicts the Passover supper when Christ becomes our lamb of sacrifice, whose blood delivers us from the angel of death, who will pass over our home and spare us. Jesus will take the bread and share with them. And then he'll take the cup and announce it to be his blood, "the blood of the covenant, poured out on behalf of many." Every Eucharist is his gift of himself on our behalf, and today's Mass celebrates his heroic and loving mercy toward us.

Cycle C
Genesis 14: 18-20 *Melchizedek, king of Salem, brought out bread and wine, and being a priest of God Most High, he blessed Abram with these words: "Blessed be Abram by God Most High, the creator of heaven and earth; and blessed be God Most High, who delivered your foes into your hand."*

Responsorial Psalm 110: 1, 2, 3, 4 *The Lord has sworn, and he will not repent: "You are a priest forever, according to the order of Melchizedek."*

1 Corinthians 11: 23-26 *I received from the Lord what I handed on to you, namely, that the Lord Jesus on the night in which he was betrayed took bread, and after he had given thanks, broke it and said, "This is my body, which is for you. Do this in remembrance of me." In the same way, after the supper, he took the cup, saying, "This cup is the new covenant in my blood. Do this, whenever you drink it, in remembrance of me."*

Luke 9: 11-17 *As sunset approached, the Twelve said to [Jesus], "Dismiss the crowd so they can go into the villages and find food, for this is certainly an out-of-the-way place." He answered, "Why do you not give them something to eat yourselves?" They replied, "We have nothing but five loaves and two fishes. Or shall we go and buy food for all these people?" (There were about five thousand men.) Jesus [told them], "Have them sit down in groups of fifty or so." Then, taking the five loaves and the two fishes, Jesus raised his eyes to heaven, pronounced a blessing over them, broke them, and gave them to his disciples for distribution to the crowd. They all ate until they had enough. What they had left, over and above, filled twelve baskets.*

Reflection:

As we read in an explanatory footnote from <u>The Catholic Study Bible</u>, "there are three main points of resemblance between Melchizedek, the prophetic type [the one who sets up the point of reference], and Christ who fulfilled this prophecy: both are kings as well as priests, both offer bread and wine to God, and both have their priesthood directly from God and not through Aaron, since neither belongs to the tribe of Levi" (Psalm 110: 4). This king of Salem will be followed centuries later by David, another king of Jerusalem, from whose line, again centuries later, will come Jesus, deliriously welcomed into his city, where he will celebrate a Passover meal (bread, wine) with his disciples, only to be handed over to the authorities later that same night. Coincidence?

In this earliest written account of the Lord's Supper (written in the late 50s, a decade before any gospel will appear), Paul will twice within two consecutive sentences report Jesus' command to "do this in remembrance." In the gospel, Jesus again calls us to action: Why don't you take care of feeding them? Our answer is so often the same: What can I do?—I'm just one person! But if we take what we have, give it to Jesus to bless it, and then take it and start sharing it...we might be surprised how far our efforts (actually, his efforts within ours) can reach.

Imagine the difference in the message if the story ended with: and there was just enough for the last person to (burp) eat the last morsel...God saw to it that the need was met, right on the button, not too much, not too little, just right. Wait a minute! Isn't it wonderful that God will always offer us way more than we need? That's how God has always been with us, prodigal, superabundant: "Give, and gifts will be given to you; a good measure, packed together, shaken down, <u>and overflowing</u> will be poured into your lap" (Luke 6: 38, emphasis added).

Today the Eucharist celebrates itself, as it were, reminding us that every Eucharist is the fulfillment of God's covenant promise to gift us with his presence, "I will be their God, and they will be my people." Our liturgy makes it clear that the meal we share is continuous with the sacrificial meals of the Old and the New Covenants. And at the same time a foretaste (remember those yummy "samples" you got/sneaked from mom in the kitchen before she took the dish out to the table?) of the everlasting banquet to come.

THE MOST SACRED HEART OF JESUS
(Friday after the second Sunday after Pentecost)

Introduction

The devotion to the Sacred Heart of Jesus obviously uses the traditional symbol of human love to bring powerfully to mind the self-sacrificing love of Jesus for his brothers and sisters. This leads us to acknowledge the insufficiency of the love that we return to him in thanks for his redeeming suffering and saving death, and as a result to apologize and try to make reparation for all our indifference and sin.

The devotion begins in answer to the wonderful apparitions of the loving Lord—his Heart ablaze with love for us—to St. Margaret Mary Alacoque, from 1673-1675. Earlier, St. John Eudes had greatly promoted the devotion to the Sacred Heart of Jesus, prompting Pope Pius XI to call him the father of the tradition, according to Rev. Peter Klein's The Catholic Source Book, p.374. Centuries later, Pius XI would prescribe the Act of Reparation to the Sacred Heart to be made on the feastday, and order a yearly public consecration of the human race on the feast of Christ the King. In 1956, Pius XII would write his encyclical on the Sacred Heart.

The basis for all this acceptance of the apparitions to St. Margaret Mary is what is rightly considered "private" revelation. Only "public" revelation has the official status of church teaching, because its source is rooted in the apostolic times, whether found in canonical writings, or in the unwritten but universally accepted Tradition coming to us from that time. (The church considers the time of public revelation to conclude with the death of the last apostle, our last historically immediate link to the teaching of Christ.)

A "private" revelation has no official standing as a church teaching, but relies on the people's acceptance of a claim that becomes recognized as valid. It is no sin to reject it, but if it leads to growth in holiness, and deepening of your devotion, you are free, and even encouraged (though never obligated), to pursue it. The easiest examples to cite are the hugely accepted apparitions of the Blessed Virgin Mary over the centuries: Guadalupe in Mexico,

Chestohowa in Poland, Montserrat in Spain, Fatima in Portugal, Lourdes in France, (on a local scale, Coromoto in Venezuela) etc. The acceptance is so overwhelming it's hard to remember that there is only the implicit approval of church authorities, not up-to-par with the written revelation in the Scriptures and the unwritten in Tradition handed down century over century.

The popular hold of the revelation of the Sacred Heart of Jesus is so powerful that it has produced the act of reparation on the feast day, the special observance of the First Friday of every month, a renewed emphasis on the Holy Hour spent in adoration of the Sacramental Presence of Jesus, expiatory temples of perpetual adoration (the famous Sacre Coeur in Paris, the equally historic Tibidabo in Barcelona), the enthronement of the Sacred Heart in the home, many practices with deep appeal to the faithful.

Scripture and Reflections

Cycle A

Deuteronomy 7: 6-11 *Moses said to the people: "You are a people sacred to the Lord, your God; he has chosen you from all the nations to be peculiarly his own. It was not because you are the largest of all nations that the Lord set his heart on you and chose you, for you are really the smallest. It was because the Lord loved you and because of his fidelity to the oath he had sworn to your fathers."*

Responsorial Psalm 103: 1-2, 3-4, 6-7, 8, 10

First letter of John 4: 7-16 *God is love. God's love was revealed in our midst in this way: he sent his only Son to the world that we might have life through him. Love consists in this: not that we have loved God, but that he has loved us and has sent his Son as an offering for our sins. Beloved, if God has loved us so, we must have the same love for one another. If we love one another God dwells in us, and his love is brought to perfection in us.*

Matthew 11: 25-30 *Jesus said: "Father, Lord of heaven and earth, to you I offer praise; for what you have hidden from the learned and the clever, you have revealed to children. Come to me, all you who are weary and find life burdensome, and I will refresh you. Take my yoke upon your shoulders, for I am gentle and humble of heart. Your souls will find rest, for my yoke is easy and my burden light."*

Reflection:

The love Jesus bears for us did not begin with him. Deep in the Old Testament we find a God who loves us with <u>hesed</u>: tender, loving kindness and mercy. Not because we have a right to his favor or have earned it in any way, but because of his fidelity to his one-sided, gratuitous covenant with us, which he keeps "down to the thousandth generation toward those who love him and keep his commandments." For St. John it's simple: if you know about love, you know about God—because God is love. And love begins not with us, but with God: he loves us, and thus enables us to return that love to him and to give it to one another as freely (undeservedly) as he has given it to us.

In Matthew's gospel, the image of the yoke is very telling, coming from a carpenter. Oxen were for the farmers of Jesus' day what a tractor is for us—they enabled a man to perform much heavier work than he could by himself. Great care was needed when fitting a yoke to the oxen. If the carpenter did not fit it properly to the contours of the animals' shoulders, it would chafe and weaken and injure the animals, instead of allowing their strength to be harnessed. Picture yourself carrying a load that God has carefully and lovingly fitted to your capacities—you know He won't ask you to do more than you can, especially if you turn and find Jesus alongside, helping you to pull the load. His yoke, the yoke we share with him, is never too heavy or difficult, because we are not left alone in our struggles. Like our faithful older brother, Jesus walks beside our every step, not doing our work for us, but ready to help when we need him.

Scripture and Reflections

Cycle B
Hosea 11: 1, 3-4, 8-9 *When Israel was a child I loved him. / It was I who taught Ephraim to walk, who took them in my arms; / I fostered them like one who raises an infant to his cheeks; / Yet, though I stooped to feed my child, they did not know that I was their healer.*

Responsorial Psalm Isaiah 12: 2-3, 4, 5-6

Ephesians 3: 8-12, 14-19 *May Christ dwell in your hearts through faith, and may charity be the root and foundation of your life.*

Thus you will be able to grasp fully the breadth and length and height and depth of Christ's love, and experience this love which surpasses all knowledge.

John 19: 31-37 *The Jews did not want to have the bodies left on the cross during the Sabbath. They asked Pilate that the legs be broken and the bodies taken away. The soldiers broke the legs of the men crucified with Jesus [but] when they came to Jesus and saw that he was already dead, they did not break his legs. One of [them] thrust a lance into his side, and immediately blood and water flowed out. (This testimony has been given by an eyewitness, and his testimony is true. He tells what he knows is true, so that you may believe.) These events took place for the fulfillment of Scripture: "Break none of his bones." There is still another Scripture passage which says: "They shall look on him whom they have pierced."*

Reflection:

What a tender image: God stooping over, teaching his people to walk, taking them in his arms, raising them to his cheeks and nuzzling them. And then his sadness when they will not acknowledge his love for them. Their failure to return his love makes him angry, but he won't give vent to his blazing anger. What does continue to blaze is his love for us, manifested to St. Margaret Mary Alacoque by the vision of his heart on fire with ardent desire. How can we remain unmoved by this God who wears his heart on his sleeve?

Paul's eloquence is inspired: with Christ dwelling in our hearts through faith, and love the foundation of our lives, we will be on the way to grasping the full breadth and length and height and depth of Christ's love for us, a love that surpasses all knowledge; it cannot come to us through our minds but only through our hearts open and responsive to his.

And finally, John reports what his own eyes have seen: that from the pierced heart of Jesus came blood and water! The first scripture quote is from Exodus, detailing the ritual killing of the lamb whose blood, spattered on their doors, will save them from the tenth and final plague, the killing of the first-born. Jesus, at his farewell Last Supper, will, according to Matthew 26, take a cup, give thanks, and give it to them, saying, "All of you must drink from it, for this is my blood, the blood of the covenant, to be poured out in behalf of many for the forgiveness of sins." In Mark 14 he tells them: "This is my blood; the blood of the covenant, to be poured out on behalf of many." And in Luke 22 he says, "This cup is the new covenant in my blood, which will be shed for you." Jesus clearly establishes the link between his saving death and the lamb's blood on their doors on their last night of slavery in Egypt.

The surprising part is the appearance of the water—so John makes a point of insisting he was there, and saw it with his own eyes. Then it hits him: as the blood provides the life in the Eucharist, so the water gave birth to that life in Baptism. Way back in chapter 4 John told the story of Jesus promising the woman at the well that he could provide living water, springing up from within! So the loving heart of Jesus provides both the birth and the sustenance of our risen life with him: Baptism and the Eucharist. What a gift, and what beautiful theological insights!

Cycle C

Ezekiel 34: 11-16 *Thus says the Lord God: I myself will look after and tend my sheep. They shall lie down on good grazing ground, and in rich pastures shall they be pastured on the mountains of Israel. I myself will pasture my sheep; I myself will give them rest, says the Lord God. The lost I will seek out, the strayed I will bring back, the injured I will bind up, the sick I will heal, shepherding them rightly.*

Responsorial Psalm 23: 1-3, 3-4, 5, 6 *The Lord is my shepherd; I shall not want. In verdant pastures he gives me repose. Beside restful waters he leads me; he refreshes my soul. Only goodness and kindness follow me all the days of my life; and I shall dwell in the house of the Lord for years to come.*

Romans 5: 5-11 *The love of God has been poured out in our hearts through the Holy Spirit who has been given to us. It is rare that anyone should lay down his life for a just man, [but] it is precisely in this that God proves his love for us: that while we were still sinners, Christ died for us.*

Luke 15: 3-7 *Jesus addressed this parable to the Pharisees and the scribes: "Who among you, if he has a hundred sheep and loses one of them, does not leave the ninety-nine and follow the lost one until* *he finds it? And when he finds it, he puts it on his shoulders in jubilation. Once arrived home, he invites friends and neighbors in and says to them, 'Rejoice with me because I have found my lost sheep.' I tell you, there will likewise be more joy in heaven over one repentant sinner than over ninety-nine righteous people who have no need to repent."*

Reflection:

Judah's kings and leaders have fallen down on the job. Yahweh himself feels the plight of his people, neglected by those he placed in charge, and promises to come down and do the job himself. The self-forgetful devotion and tender care of a good shepherd is what his people need, and through Ezekiel, God promises to do the job right. "If you want the job done right, you've gotta do it yourself!" was true even then.

David, the Shepherd-King, sings the beautiful image of God as his Shepherd, pasturing, leading, protecting. Little did we suspect that when Jesus claimed, "I am the good shepherd" he was actually making a claim on divinity, carrying out Yahweh's own chosen task (John 10).

The Sacred Heart devotion gratefully acknowledges Christ's love for us sinners. Paul's message here, once again employing baptismal verbiage (God's love "poured" into our hearts through the Holy Spirit), makes a special point. If these were prize sheep, all fed and groomed for tomorrow's 4-H exhibition, you could see the shepherd standing up to the wolf, or whatever else threatened them. The remarkable thing about this shepherd is that the sheep he's willing to give up his life for...are a bunch a scraggly, sickly, unkempt losers! "While we were still sinners, Christ died for us." Thank you, Jesus!

What a comforting image Luke presents: the sinner, the lamb that wanders off and ends up lost and needing help to return to safety, will be sought after until it's found and brought back—on the shepherd's shoulders (poor dumb little thing, it's all tired out). It's telling that right after he commissions the Twelve (Matthew 10: 1-4) Jesus sends them out, instructing them, "Go to the lost sheep of the house of Israel" (10:6). And His shepherd-role was taken to heart by the early church. It has been reported that, in the catacombs where we brought our beloved deceased while we were still an underground church (get it?), the image of Jesus found most often carved into the stone is that of a shepherd carrying a lamb on his shoulders. This is the same tender concern of a loving, saving Jesus for his straying, sin-weakened brothers and sisters, coming near to warm our hearts with the blaze of his great love for us visible in his Sacred Heart. Thank you, Jesus!

Seven
IT ALL COMES TOGETHER

The Continuum: Lent, Triduum, Mystagogia—
Ash Wednesday to Pentecost Sunday

L ooking at the Easter Triduum in the context of our cultural values, we have to ask ourselves if we as a Christian community, as a family, have a statement to make about this sacred time. Do our high holy days have an effective significance, or do they fall below the level of our secular celebrations of Labor Day or the Fourth of July? Do we have the commitment to be a sign of contradiction for just a few days a year? Our example can close cash registers, turn off car ignitions and televisions, put the Internet on hold, give those aching carpal-tunnels some ease, and in general reduce the endless noise and rush of American society.

These should be days when it would be really gross of us to contribute to the Gross National Product.

In Fr. Siwek's 1979 liturgical magaine article "Easter Triduum–Spirit and Observance" we read: "If we tell ourselves the Easter Triduum is the highlight of the liturgical year and go on with business as usual then we are just fooling ourselves. Good Friday is just another T.G.I.F." Let's face it: Easter Sunday aside, the Triduum doesn't hold a candle (get it?) to Thanksgiving, which is really a combination of civic and mostly pro forma religious observances, with little or no liturgical standing, that is nonetheless enjoyed almost universally in our culture.

Imagine the powerful effect of a few days when the entire Christian community exercises its faith in unity. Not somber days, but a time of peace and quiet. Just think: no radios blaring, no soap operas or quiz shows or ESPN. Set free from these invisible chains, we would suddenly find the time to visit old friends or relatives (who, after getting over the shock, might even enjoy spending some time with us). We could dust off our Bibles and read a gospel, go to the liturgies of the Sacred Triduum (inviting and bringing those surprised relatives/old friends), and reflect on the meaning of Christ's dying and rising for ourselves and our hectic culture. We could re-examine our marriages and/or family relationships, make time for getting together with friends, write letters, try not to rush anywhere, take a nap! One very appropriate outdoor activity is getting out of our daily routine and taking a hike. The new life of springtime is a reflection of the paschal mystery of death and rebirth. All creation around us, if we just stop and check it out, is renewed through the death and resurrection of the Lord. These days should be a retreat in the best sense of the word.

The Easter Triduum has in fact been the second stage of what could be called the church's retreat, as James Empereur, S.J., points out in his article "The Easter Triduum" (p. 300, The New Dictionary of Theology, Michael Glazier, Inc.). Ash Wednesday began the Church's first period of special reflection, the season of Lent. A time to fast so as to purify our hearts, to control our desires so as to be able to show to those in need God's goodness to ourselves, to be in solidarity with the catechumens preparing to join the church; a time to engage in reconciliation, that life-giving forgiveness which ideally takes place in the community, that calls to mind the meaning and power of Baptism, and that leads to sharing in the Eucharist.

And the great fifty days that lie ahead (Pentecost, a week of weeks) offer the newly received members of the community some time for steeping in the juices of Easter. The period was called in Greek the mystagogia, a time for entering more deeply into the teachings offered them in their Lenten preparation, so that the lessons of Lent can be incorporated, slowly and effectively, into a mature Christian way of life. This third and final stage culminates in God's sending of the Holy Spirit, with Jesus already off in the wings as of his Ascension ten days before. We're on our own! The training wheels come off. With the sending of the Holy

Spirit, both the creative mission of the Father, and the redeeming mission of the Son, are now completed and we take over the controls, with the felt presence of the Spirit to guide us in the way of sanctification.

In conclusion (so it's come to this...):

Gentle Reader,

Farewell. Thank you for letting me share all this with you. I pray that God might use it to promote his growth and love and desires in you. And I ask you to pray also: ask God to keep reminding me that the word on the lips (or fingertips, as I sit and type) is nothing until it becomes the action on the hands. "Some of the seed looked/sounded good, but it fell by the wayside and never produced anything but noise—it just withered and died." Ouch. So please keep me in your prayers, as I do you in mine. Thank you. And thank you, Jesus!